1,001

THINGS TO DO WHEN
THERE'S NOTHING TO DO

1,001

THINGS TO DO WHEN
THERE'S NOTHING TO DO

LOUISE COLLIGAN AND LINDA ABER

SCHOLASTIC INC.
New York Toronto London Auckland Sydney

ISBN 0-590-46359-4

12 11 10 9 8 7 6 5 4 3 2   4 5 6 7 8/9

Printed in the U.S.A.   40

First Scholastic printing, May 1994

(93-94)

Dedicated to
Corey and Kip Aber
and Deirdre Colligan

CONTENTS

Introduction: When Boredom Strikes,
Strike Back! 1
Spring Things to Do 3
Too Hot — *Not!* 4
Cloudy Beach Day 9
Fall into Fun 10
It's Snowing! It's Snowing! 11
School Lunch Table 14
Make the Best of Recess 15
The Wheel Thing 17
Feeling Jumpy 20
Third Rainy Weekend in a Row 22
No Friends, Nothing to Do 25
Missing Friends 27
Here's the Friend, Where's the Fun? 28
Lots of Friends, Nothing to Do 29
Friendly Solutions to Friendly Fights 32
Join the Club! 33
Home Alone 37
Let's Party! 40
Nothing to Do in This Neighborhood 42
Nothing to Do in This Town 45
Nothing to Do on This Planet! 47
Who's New? You! 49
Sick of Being Homesick 52
Sick of Being Sick 53

Grounded! 56
Change a No to a Yes 57
Stress Busters 59
More Things to Do on Your Own 61
Commercial-Break Games 64
After Dinner, Before Bed 66
Lights Out, Can't Sleep 67
Up Too Early, and No One Else Is
    Awake Yet 69
Stormy Nights, Stormy Lights 72
Your Wallet's Empty, and Everybody's
    Going to the Movies 76
You Like Toddlers, but You're Too Young
    to Baby-sit Alone 77
Must Raise Cash for Holiday Shopping 79
The Best Gifts in Life Are Free 80
Best Friends — Must Raise Cash
    Together 82
No Money for Summer Vacation 83
Have a Little Money, Need More 85
To Grandmother's House We Go 86
Go Play With Your Cousins 87
So Much to Talk About 90
On the Sidelines 91
Waiting on Tables 93
Long Lines — The Wait You Love
    to Hate 94
Busy on the Bus 96
Car Pool Capers 99
Backseat Blues 100

City Sidewalks, Busy Sidewalks 103

What's in Store? 105

While Strolling Through the Park
   One Day 106

See 'em in the Museum 108

Room with a View 110

Tired of Your Room? 111

Need a New Look? 114

Hacking Around on Your Computer 115

Picture This 116

When There's Nothing to Do, Learn
   Something New 118

One Thing Leads to Another 120

Be a Collecto-Maniac! 122

An Empty Jar Can Be Full of Fun 127

Snack Attack! 130

Twisted Tongue Twisters to Tell 133

Ridiculous Riddles to Ask 134

Funniest Body Tricks to Play 135

Practical Jokes That Get 'em
   Every Time 138

Quick Tricks for Last Licks 139

The Boredom-Buster Bag 141

What *Not* to Do if You're Superstitious 142

Ways to Do Nothing When There's
   Nothing to Do 143

10 of *Your* Best Ideas of What to Do 145

1,001

THINGS TO DO WHEN
THERE'S NOTHING TO DO

WHEN BOREDOM STRIKES, STRIKE BACK!

What? You say you're bored? Nothing to do and no one to do nothing with? Well, nothing to worry about either. Here are 1,001 interesting, creative suggestions to help you find fun wherever you are, whomever you're with, and no matter what you have or don't have with you. This book is packed with ways to beat the blahs that boredom brings. You never know when boredom may strike, but with this book you'll always be ready to strike back!

1

SPRING THINGS TO DO

Spring is here! It's time to start fresh. Here are some new boredom beaters just for this season.

1 **Have a first-flower contest.** See who can spot the first buds coming up.
2 **Look for the first robin of spring.** Mark your calendar the day you spot it.
3 **Look for bird eggshells.** Baby birds are sure to be nearby. Don't touch baby birds, though, or the mother won't either.
4 **Hang up a bird feeder.** Watch the birds gather there.
5 **Build a birdhouse.** Hang it in a tree and watch for the new neighbors!
6 **Imitate bird songs.** If you start growing feathers, you've probably practiced too much!
7 **Fly a kite.**
8 **Have a Spring Festival in your neighborhood.** Start with a parade of bike riders down your street, followed by a neighborhood volleyball game, and a bring-your-own-basket picnic.
9 **Hang up wind chimes.**
10 **Feed ducks and geese at a nearby pond.**
11 **Go to the zoo.** Look at all the newborns.
12 **Buy your first ice-cream cone of the season.** This will get you in training for summer!

13 Invent a cure for spring fever.

14 Ask your teacher if you can have class outside.

15 **Go to a garage sale.** Make a deal with yourself not to spend more than a dollar.

16 **Have a carnival.** Plan carnival games such as ringtoss, penny pitch, bowling-pin knock-down, Velcro darts, and beanbag toss. Invite everyone you know.

17 **Read the section called The Wheel Thing.** Pick a few games to do with your friends on your bikes, Rollerblades, roller skates, or skateboards.

18 **Look for caterpillars.** Keep them in a jar with grass. Punch holes in the top of the jar. Watch them closely for a while. Let them go so they can turn into summer's butterflies.

19 **Play a trick on your family.** After you let your caterpillar go, put the jar sideways on the kitchen counter or in the bathroom — without the lid.

 # TOO HOT — *NOT!*

On hot summer days, lather on the sunscreen and beat the heat with these hot tips for keeping cool.

20 **Find out if you really can fry an egg on the sidewalk on a hot day.**

21 **Make a rainbow.** With the sun behind you, water the garden or the sidewalk with a fine spray. See, there it is!

22 **Have a water balloon fight.**

23 **Play "Hose Tag" or "Squirt Bottle Tag."**

24 **Do a "rain dance."** Have a show of creative dances or gymnastic movements under the spray of a sprinkler.

25 **Play "Hose Limbo."** One person holds the hose up high with a steady stream of water flowing. The other person goes under the stream once. The stream is lowered a little more each turn until the person doing the ducking-under gets wet.

26 **Play "Sprinkler Jump."** Using a sprinkler that goes around in a circle, wait for the spray to come to you and jump over the water. Set a record for the number of jumps. Then try to beat your own record.

27 **Play a sport near a sprinkler.**

28 **Watch birds take a shower.** Prop the garden hose up in the tree branches and turn on a fine spray of water.

29 **Set up a Swing-and-Sprinkle.** Put the sprinkler in a place where it will sprinkle you as you go back and forth on a swing.

30 **Make a water slide.** Turn the hose on and let the water run down the slide. Slide down — in your bathing suit, of course!

31 **Have a water fight.** Start a heated argument

with a friend. You'll cool off faster than you ever did before!

32 Play in your old kiddie pool. Do what you haven't done in years — using a plastic baby pool or large tub of water, float boats, play with your old rubber ducks, blow bubbles underwater.

33 Play pool. Do indoor things outdoors while sitting in the kiddie pool. Eat your lunch, do a crossword puzzle, read a book.

34 Put the kiddie pool at the bottom of a slide. Land with a splash!

35 Paint your body. All you need are a garden hose, paintbrushes, watercolor paints, and your body. Paint "tattoos" on your arms, stripes on your legs, or paint yourself completely blue — or any color you like! Then cool down as you wash the paint off with a hose.

36 If you're at a pool, dive for pennies.

37 Go to the beach. Who says you can't? Set up your beach umbrella right there in your yard or at the local park. Spread out a beach blanket under the shade of the umbrella and do a little summer reading. When you get hot, run cold water over the insides of your wrists. When you cool your pulse points your whole body cools off.

38 Have a melt-off contest. Lie on a beach towel. Put one ice cube on your chest and one on your stomach. See which one melts first. Or try competing against your friends — who can melt an ice cube the fastest? Who can make it last the longest?

39 **Sit in deep shade.** Close your eyes. Don't move. See how many cool, cold, or *frozen* things you can think of in five minutes. Make it a contest with a friend.

40 **Make a "snow angel" without the snow.** Spread yourself out on the grass so whatever air there is can flow all around you.

41 **Hats on!** You know that weird hat your great-uncle gave you? Put it on. Hats keep you cool when you're out in the hot sun.

42 **Make a glass of real lemonade.** Make fresh lemonade using the juice of one lemon, sugar to taste, and 8 ounces of water. Add ice and drink.

43 **Cool off with ice packs.** Freeze juice boxes and hold them against your forehead and neck. When you feel cooler, stick the straw in the box and drink the juice.

44 **Turn on the juice.** Make ice pops from whatever fruit juices you have in the house.

45 **Spritz yourself.** Keep a spray bottle of water in the refrigerator. Take it along with you when you play outside.

46 **Make frozen fruit.** Freeze grapes, strawberries, mushed up watermelon, or bananas. They'll be just right in about an hour.

47 **Make your own ice-cream sandwich.** Soften

some ice cream just a little. Spread it between two chocolate chip cookies. Freeze it for just 20 minutes, and it's ready.

48 **Make ice-cream soup.** Let ice cream melt a little. Add some berries. Eat it outside under a shady tree.

49 **Eat icy cold watermelon.** Save the seeds and have a seed-spitting contest to see how far you can spit them. Outdoors, of course!

50 **Keep frosty glasses in the freezer.** Drink out of them when you're thirsty.

51 **Put bubble mix in the fridge.** Pour into a big pan. Shape a wire coat hanger into a big loop. Blow huge bubbles then walk into them.

52 **Scrub-a-dub!** Have a car wash for your parents and neighbors. Wear a bathing suit while you're working. Cool down while making some cool cash!

53 **Teatime.** Put fresh water in a clean glass vase or large jar. Add a few tea bags. Put out in the sun for three hours. Add ice and share with friends and family on a hot day.

54 **Have a snowball fight.** Use the snowballs you froze in #76. Quick, before they melt!

CLOUDY BEACH DAY

A gray day at the beach can still be a great day at the beach. Here's how to brighten a cloudy day!

55 **Make sand paintings.** Get a few empty jars and some food dye. Pour sand and a few drops of dye into each jar and mix. Flatten a section of sand and sprinkle on the colored sand in pretty patterns.

56 **Sand leftovers.** Layer the leftover colored sand in one of the jars. Use the jar as a pretty desktop paperweight.

57 **Organize a sand monster building contest.** Ask everyone to come at low tide when there's plenty of wet sand.

58 **Make swirl art.** Make swirly patterns with glue on a piece of white posterboard. Sprinkle with colored sand and let dry.

59 **Make shell figures as souvenirs.** You know — the ones with the googly eyes and cork hats. Get your craft supplies and make your own for free.

60 **Bring a powerful magnet to search for coins at the beach.**

61 **Collect soda cans on the beach and redeem them.** Treat yourself to an ice-cream cone. Eat it as you walk along the empty beach.

62 **Write messages and greetings in the wet sand.**

Lie next to the message. Have someone take your picture. You now have a supply of any-occasion photo greeting cards.

☆ **FALL INTO FUN**

If autumn leaves you falling asleep with boredom, fall for these ideas!

63 **Go apple picking.** Check the newspaper or yellow pages in the phone book for nearby farms or orchards. Picking apples makes eating them even more fun!

64 **Go on a tailgate picnic.** Just because it's fall doesn't mean it's time to put away the family picnic basket. On a crisp fall day, pack a picnic to eat during intermission at a local soccer, field hockey, or football game.

65 **When the neighborhood is full of leaves, have a scarecrow contest.** Send a flyer around asking your neighbors to stuff some of their old clothes with all those leaves at the curb, and display the "scarecrows" on their porches or in their windows. Set a deadline right before Halloween. Pick some judges to pick the scariest, silliest, or sweetest scarecrow that never scared anyone away!

66 **Catch apples.** Tie strings to the stems of two apples. Hang the strings and apples from a tree branch. Challenge a friend to an apple-catching contest. Start the apples swinging just slightly. With hands behind your backs, try to catch the apples in your teeth.

67 **Paint a pumpkin you've picked or bought.** Using acrylic paints, paint a jack-o'-lantern face on one side. Then on Halloween Day, carve the other side and put your candle-lit jack-o'-lantern out to greet trick-or-treaters.

68 **Think spring.** Start a tulip or daffodil bulb-planting service. Let neighbors know you're available to dig holes and plant bulbs for a small fee. Any gardening book will tell you just how deep to dig and what to do.

69 **Start a fall cleanup service.** Even people who love gardening hate pulling up faded flowers and plants. Brighten their fall and do it for them. All you need are some trash bags and a rake.

70 **Go for a moonlight walk.** Find out when the full moons will occur in October and November (when the moon is at its fullest of the year). Bring along hot cider and some doughnuts.

✍ IT'S SNOWING! IT'S SNOWING!

Everyone knows what to do on snow days. Go outside and play in it! Here are some great ways to really have a snowball!

71 Shovel. The driveway, the sidewalk, the front steps. Use the piles of snow for the foundation of a snow fort.

72 Build a snow fort. Make the wall high enough to hide behind. Make windows in the wall so you can see your friend in the other snow fort.

73 Build a snow fence around your yard.

74 Make snowballs by the bunch. Pile them up and have them ready for target practice or just a good, old-fashioned snowball fight.

75 Have a snowball contest. See who can make the most gigantic snowball. Take a picture. Then cut into the snowball and make a snow throne to sit on.

76 Freeze some snowballs. You'll need them on a hot July day when you wish you could have a snowball fight!

77 Play "Snowball Tag."

78 Track animal footprints in the snow. See where they lead you.

79 Have a Snowman Fashion Show. Dress up your snow people in the latest styles and have a contest to see which one looks the most fashionable.

80 Build a few snowmen right outside a window, looking in. From inside the house you'll feel surrounded by guardian snowmen.

81 Make snow sculptures. Break out of the usual snowman mold. Make snow animals, snow things, or just a giant tower.

82 Have a snow castle contest on your street.

83 Make a snow maze. Use your entire yard. Create walls and pathways leading nowhere. Make only one way out. Invite your friends over to get lost!

84 Make a pink snowman for a change. Use food dye or water-based paints to dye the snow.

85 Go sledding. Race down in saucers, garbage-can lids, a flattened cardboard box, or even a trash bag. Sleds are good for sledding, too!

86 Go snow rolling. Bundle up and have a rolling race down the hill.

87 Make snow angels. Lie flat on your back in freshly fallen snow. Spread your arms and legs out and move them back and forth to make an angel shape.

88 Look at snowflakes close up. Catch a snowflake on a piece of cold glass. Look at it under a microscope or powerful magnifying glass.

89 Bury a "treasure" in the deepest snowbank. Remember where you buried it and see how long it takes for your treasure to show up again.

90 Sell hot chocolate. Go out with friends and a couple of thermoses of hot chocolate and some cups. Sell hot chocolate to snow shovelers, snow plowers, and frosty snowball fighters.

91 Have a picnic in the snow.

92 Have a marshmallow hunt. Hide marshmallows around in the snow. The one who finds the most wins a cup of hot chocolate topped with fresh marshmallows (not the ones from the outside).

93 **Make snow sundaes with favorite toppings.**

94 **Have a winter barbecue.** With help from a grown-up, toast marshmallows or S'Mores (graham crackers, chocolate bar or chocolate bits, marshmallows) over the grill.

95 **Play "Cat's Cradle."** Eskimos invented this game to "catch" the summer sun in the string cradle so it wouldn't set so fast in winter.

SCHOOL LUNCH TABLE

Whoever said you shouldn't play with your food hasn't been in a school cafeteria lately. Pass the time inventing new ways to fix up the same old lunchroom food.

96 **Invent new salads at the salad bar.**

97 **Make food people.** Use a fork for the body. Spear fruit or vegetable chunks for the head. Decorate with peas and toothpicks.

98 **Designate Backwards Lunch Day.** Eat dessert first.

99 **Make a Pac-Man tomato.** Cut a slice across the middle of a cherry tomato. Make it talk. "Pass the salt, please." (Do this over a plate!)

100 Once a week, eat at a different lunch table. You might make new friends, and the view will be different.

101 Take a poll of favorites and not-so-favorite foods. Give the results to the cafeteria manager.

102 Designate Healthy Lunch Day. Try the healthiest foods on the menu.

103 Have a Fortune Cookie Day. Ask each friend to write a fortune on a piece of paper. Collect, mix, distribute, and read them out loud at dessert time.

104 Have a Funny Lunch Day. Tell everyone to share jokes around the lunch table.

❤ **MAKE THE BEST OF RECESS**

It's never long enough, but recess can be fun enough if you have these ideas in mind.

105 Search for lost coins on the playground or field. Look carefully everywhere you walk. You're sure to find pennies, nickels, dimes, and other coins that fell out of kids' pockets.

106 Organize a relay race. Divide the group into two teams. Form two lines. Have the first runner of each line race down to a designated mark and back to tag the next runner in his line. First line to finish wins.

107 Read a book you don't have to read.

108 **Start a Recess Players Club.** Every day put on a talent show, a short skit, or any kind of act for the rest of the kids out for recess.

109 **Have a Recess Treasure Hunt.** Ask the recess teacher to hide some object. Then let the group spread out and search.

110 **Play checkers.** Set up several games at a time and have a recess tournament. Continue all the way to play-offs until you have a checkers champion.

111 **Be a Recess Reporter.** Make notes about things that happen at recess. Write them up as news stories and submit them to the school newspaper.

112 **Make up a new game.** Start with a ball and make up a new kind of ball game.

113 **Plan a weeks' worth of special recess days.** Designate a Ball Day, a Jump Rope Day, a Jacks Day, a Board Game Day, or any other kind of day, when kids bring in a certain type of game to share with other kids. Have play-offs, championships, or just plain old fun with whatever everyone brings in.

114 **Start a Clapping-Rapping Group.** Stand in a circle so that you can clap hands with the person on either side of you. Make up a rap rhyme that goes with the clapping.

115 **Have contests for everything.** Staring contest,

continuous talking contest, don't-make-me-laugh contest, funniest face contest, longest handstand contest, loudest whistling contest . . .

THE WHEEL THING

Almost anything you can do on foot is more fun on wheels. Try these "wheely" good games and turn your life around.

116 **Can it.** Collect about twenty soda cans, a timer, and lots of friends with their wheels (bikes, skates, or skateboards). Space out the soda cans in a squiggly, snakey slalom course along the driveway, parking lot, road, or sidewalk where you ride. Time each other to see how fast you can get through the slalom. Add on two seconds for each knocked-down can.

117 **Chalk it up.** All the soda cans gone to the recycling center? Draw a long, curvy, 12-inch-wide slalom course with chalk. See who can get through the course fastest without smudging the chalk.

118 **Have a snail race.** See who can get through the slalom courses as *slowly* as possible on a bike. Sounds easy. *NOT!*

119 **Organize a Bike-Detailing Day.** Do it for money or do it for free. You'll need a couple of buckets of soapy and clean water, sandpaper for rust, chrome polish for handlebars and tire rims, some rags, and touch-up metallic paints in different colors. Add a few decals, and you'll turn old wheels into hot wheels.

120 Hold a Bike Clinic. Get a kids' bike book out of the library. Read up on three simple things: inflating tires, fixing a flat, and raising the seat. Get your tools, pump, and biking buddies together for a fix-up session.

121 Design a hot helmet that's cool. It's hot, it's heavy, it's your dumb helmet. But not for long. Turn your hot helmet into a *HOT!!!* one with neon stickers, paints, and decals.

122 Customize your skateboard. If you're tired of your skateboard — or it's your skateboard that's a little tired — jazz it up with spray paints and decals. Work out your design on paper first.

123 Get a leg up. Skate with one leg out in front of you for as long as you can go. If friends are around, make it a contest. Do a one-legged slalom.

124 Have a barrel of laughs while you're skating. Take a half dozen soda cans and line them up like a row of barrels. See how many you and your friends can jump over without hitting any.

125 Don't fight about whether to skateboard or play ball. Do both! Play full court outdoor basketball, but do it on skateboards. Balance yourself for foul shots by putting one foot on the ground.

126 Pucker up. Play street hockey with skateboards for a change instead of roller skates.

127 Play a wheel game of tag. Play tag on skates or skateboards.

128 Spiral Race. Draw a spiral chalk course and try to stay *on* the lines with your wheels.

129 Organize a scavenger hunt — on wheels. Scout a course in your neighborhood, then ask your riding friends to check a list of things you find — like the color of a house at a certain address, initials carved in a certain tree, the color of flowers in someone's front yard, the number of windows at a house down the block, and so on. The winner designs the next scavenger hunt.

130 Play basketball with wastebaskets. Send all your friends home to empty one or two wastebaskets each. Set up the wastebaskets about 10 feet apart in a straight line. Mark a start and finish line with a chalk line about 5 feet before and after the line of baskets. Each cyclist, skateboarder, or skater races to drop a tennis ball into each basket while weaving in and out of the lines.

131 Lose your marbles. Set up this game if someone thinks the wastebasket game is too easy. This time use small food cans and marbles instead of wastebaskets and a tennis ball. Racers try to drop a teeny, tiny marble into a teeny, tiny can.

132 Have an Egg-in-Spoon Race on wheels. Don't forget to bring a bucket of soapy water along with the eggs and spoons to wash away the goo.

133 Head for the hills. Have an uphill bike race for a change. Private driveways, and school or no-car park roadways are safe places to try this.

134 Balance the books. Have a contest to see how far you and your friends can bike ride, skateboard, or roller skate with a book on your head.

135 Wheel money. Sooner or later it happens. The wheels you loved two years ago are rusty, dusty, and musty. Everyone else seems to be zooming by on the latest shiny, neon-decorated machines. You want one of those. How can you get one? Put those good old wheels to work. Start a doughnut delivery service on weekend mornings. Sign people up on Friday. If you're allowed to ride your wheels to local stores, the library, or the post office, take orders for errands. Take your wheels around town to find redeemable cans. Or ride around and post ads for selling your wheels and put the money toward new wheels.

 # FEELING JUMPY

The best cure for jumpiness is — guess what — jumping! Get out that old jump rope that someone gave you for your birthday. Twirl those hands, stomp those feet, and jump for joy.

136 Jump rope on one foot.

137 Cross your ankles and jump.

138 Tap-dance between jumps.

139 Jump twice for every turn.

140 Duck skip. Jump in a crouched position.

141 Spin around as you jump rope.

142 Play "Footsies." Jump with feet together on one turn of the rope then feet apart on the next.

143 Play "Crossie." Cross your arms at the elbow as the rope comes down in front of you. Uncross your arms to bring the rope back up behind you.

144 Use your head (and shoulders, knees and toes, knees and toes). Have two other players turn the rope at each end and repeat the verse in the song: "Head and shoulders, knees and toes, knees and toes," etc. Touch your body as you jump.

145 Watch out for snakes. Two kids wriggle each end of the rope along the ground. Jumpers take turns jumping back and forth along the length of the wriggling rope without getting "bitten" (touching the rope).

146 Watch your step. Two kids hold a rope tight at each end so the rope is a few inches above the ground. Jumpers take turns jumping over. The rope is raised several inches higher for each round.

147 Jump and wriggle. Same as #146 only the kids holding the rope wriggle it as kids jump over.

148 **Slice the rope.** Someone holds the rope tight at each end but "slices" the air with the rope by snapping it up and down repeatedly. Jumpers try to jump over between "slices."

149 **Switch places.** A kid at each end holds the rope a foot off the ground and sways it. Two other kids facing each other on the same side try to jump over the rope at the same time. One of the kids holding the rope calls out "Switch!" and the two jumpers have to switch places in midair yet land and keep jumping on the same side.

THIRD RAINY WEEKEND IN A ROW

Is the weather channel playing reruns? Don't just sit there waiting for the skies to clear. Make your own fun and sun.

150 **Have a beach party indoors.** Ask everyone to put on his or her bathing suit. Spread a blanket on the floor. Pack a picnic. Take all the lamp shades off and turn up the lights. Borrow your parents' Beach Boys music, and have an indoor day at the beach.

151 **If a big storm's blowing, it's time for a spooky**

book. Take some books with creepy titles out of the library. Keep a flashlight ready in case the lights go out.

152 **Start a rainy day service in the neighborhood.** Entertain little kids with activities #504, #505, and #507. Offer to weed neighbors' lawns and gardens. Weeds come right up on rainy days. Run errands for people who hate to go out in the rain.

153 **Give yourself a head start.** Get a jump on things you'll be too busy to do later on. Read an extra chapter in a schoolbook. Make out mailing labels for holiday, birthday, and thank-you cards. Make a list of what you want to be for Halloween. Design some greeting cards. Plan a gift list for your favorite people. (Check out some great gift ideas: #530–#547.)

154 **Hold a movie festival.** If you have a VCR, call up friends to get together for a movie fest. Each person brings a favorite tape and a favorite snack food. You won't have to wait in line, and you won't have to worry about a tall person sitting in front of you!

155 **Organize your loose photos.** Put them in groups like friends, pets, holidays, summer, birthdays, big events, vacations. Then go do something fun you saw in one of the pictures.

156 **Play "Balloon Volleyball" with one friend or a bunch.** Blow up a balloon. String a length of masking tape or string across the middle of a big room. Divide into equal teams. Send the balloon up and toss it over the tape or string.

If there's no thunder or lightning try these:

157 **Make a big splash.** Get out old clothes, rubber boots, rain jacket, or poncho. Play some of your usual outdoor games in the rain!

158 **Make a bigger splash.** If it's warm enough, play the same games in your *bathing suit*!

159 **Soap up the family car.** You won't need a hose to rinse it, and everybody'll be glad to get the car clean.

160 **Go to the local playground.** For a change, you won't have to wait to use the most popular equipment.

161 **Go for a walk.** Look for worms. Make faces at your reflection in the puddles. Puddle jump. If it's a warm, walk barefoot in the grass.

162 **Take your little sister or brother for a walk in your neighborhood.** Do the same things as in #506, #515, and #516. You'll have twice the fun.

163 **Make mud pies.** It's a mess, but it's lots of fun. Or stay dry and make a Mississippi Mud Pie indoors. Pour softened chocolate ice cream into a prebaked graham cracker crust. Stir in crumbled cookies or brownies. Put in the freezer. Count raindrops for two hours. Go have a piece of pie.

164 **Collect rain.** No, not for your collection, for your

hair. Rainwater makes your hair soft and shiny.
Use it to rinse your hair after a shampoo.

✏ NO FRIENDS, NOTHING TO DO

Your friends are away, and you're stuck at home.
No reason to mope — you can cheer yourself up!

165 **When close friends are away, get new ones!**
Call up kids you'd like to know better. You know
who they are — the ones you see at soccer or
baseball practice, band, or dance lessons. Invite
one of them over. When your old friends get back,
add your new friend to the group.

166 **Do something you enjoy that your friends don't.**
Watch that movie you secretly like. Wear an
outfit you usually don't wear around your friends.
Listen to music your friends are tired of.

167 **Baby yourself.** Be a little kid for an hour or two.
Do something most of your friends might consider
babyish. Get out some old toys. Listen to kiddie
tapes. Read picture books. Watch cartoons. Go
down a slide.

168 **Make a wish list.** List all the experiences you
hope to have or things you'd like to own. (Then
turn to #521–#529 or #556–#572 and earn the
money to buy them!)

169 **Do one Be-Good-to-Yourself Activity every day**

your friends are gone. Eat your favorite food. Wear your favorite clothes. Get into your favorite hobby or collection.

170 **Design a door poster for your room.** Get some poster board and draw your name in huge fancy letters. Decorate with spangles, sequins, and neon colors. Hang the poster on the door.

171 **Make like an ant.** Feel like crawling into an ant hole until your friends get back? Watch how an ant does it. Lay out some sugar or cookie crumbs near an ant hole. Then watch how they get their "take-out" food down the hole.

172 **Think you're alone? Think again.** On a summer day, check under doormats, planters, rocks, and logs. None of those critters got to go on vacation, either!

173 **Follow the neighborhood cat.** Find out where *he* goes when he's bored.

174 **Follow a snail trail.** If you're really bored, and have *lots* of time, trail a snail. Pour powder on their slimy tracks and see where they lead.

175 **Take a trip.** With your parents' permission, ride whatever bus goes through your town. Take it to the end of the line, then turn around and come back. Are your friends home yet?

176 **Teach yourself one new skill.** See #818–#852.

MISSING FRIENDS

Pass the time with "Thinking-of-You" projects for when your sidekick gets back.

177   **Make a friendship bracelet.** Put it in a "Welcome Back" envelope and stick it under the front door of your friend's house.

178   **Clip favorite comic strips, local news, and sports news while your friend is gone.** Add your own news reports about what's been going on in the neighborhood.

179   **Make a "Welcome Home" banner.** Get it autographed by friends who didn't go away. Tape it over your friend's front door right before he or she comes back.

180   **Make a friendship collage.** Go through magazines and photos. Cut out pictures of people, places, activities, and great stuff you know your friend likes. Cut out letters to spell out his or her name. Arrange everything in a plastic box frame or just on a piece of construction paper. Now you have a great present to give when your friend gets back.

181   **Look up your friend's name in a name book.** You can find one at the local library. With your fanciest markers and lettering, design a small card, suitable for display, of your friend's name and its meaning.

182 **Make a Friend-in-a-Jar.** Fill a glass jar with colored slips of paper with messages about why you like your friend: *Honest, Friendly, Funny, Dependable, Nice, Kind, Sincere, Cute, Athletic,* or anything else that fits. Label the jar FRIEND-IN-A-JAR. Cover the lid with a circle of fabric and tie it on with pretty yarn.

183 **Tape it!** Make a funny tape of what you've been doing while your friend's away.

HERE'S THE FRIEND, WHERE'S THE FUN?

You've found one other lonely soul to come over and spend the day with you. Now what?

184 **Take turns leading each other on blindfolded walks around the neighborhood.** Try to guess where you are.

185 **Draw caricatures or silhouettes of each other.**

186 **Make up a spy kit.** Cut out small holes in a newspaper so you can watch someone while pretending to read the paper. Tape a mirror inside a book so you can "read" and watch someone behind you. Go for a walk and try it out.

187 **Make up an obstacle course.** Pretend you're spies in training. Try to crawl through the course without making a sound or disturbing the obstacles. The obstacles can be a row of cans, dry sticks, leaves, or newspapers.

188 **"Shadow" passersby.** See how close and how far you can follow someone without being spotted.

189 **Put together an "undercover" outfit.** Raid the attic and see if you and your friend can design outfits that will make you unrecognizable in your own neighborhood.

190 **Jump for joy.** Get out your jump rope and jump side by side with your friend.

191 **Jump together.** Start jumping rope alone. Then have your friend jump in with you, and jump together.

☆ # LOTS OF FRIENDS, NOTHING TO DO

If two heads are supposed to be better than one, how come six, or eight, or ten of you are dying of boredom? Don't just sit there like a bunch of bumps on a log. Get going with these crowd pleasers.

192 **Organize a lending library.** Have every kid bring two to three books they've read and liked to the "library" (somebody's basement, room, garage, lawn). Set up a two-week sign-out system, then do it again!

193 **Organize a lending toy store.** Same as #192 only lend toys.

194 **Hold a songfest.** Make a tape of one or two bars of popular songs. Then have kids guess and sing the whole song.

195 **Play daytime "Camouflage Hide-and-Seek."** Send everyone home and tell them to come back in green, brown, or tan play clothes (or white if there's a lot of snow around). Then play hide-and-seek.

196 **Play "Camouflage Hide-and-Seek" after dark.** Wear your darkest clothes and hide in different yards.

197 **Guess who?** One person has to think of someone everyone knows. The other kids ask questions: If this person were an animal, color, food, jewel, flower, tree, or bird, which one would he or she be?

198 **Hide ten things around the neighborhood.** Then make a list of what you hid. Hand it out so everyone can go on a scavenger hunt. The winner gets to organize the next hunt.

199 **Use the photos you can make in #806 to organize a neighborhood scavenger hunt.**

200 **Lineup.** Blindfold one person. The others stand

in a lineup. The blindfolded person has to touch one part of each person — a hand, a nose, hair, a shoe — then guess who the person is.

201 **Play "People-Eating Dragon."** Line up two or three kids to form a "dragon" by joining arms with each other. They run together without letting go and surround one of the kids who's not in the "dragon." Getting caught means joining the dragon and encircling the next victim, until everyone has been "eaten" by the dragon.

202 **Jump in.** Start jumping rope and have a friend jump in, then jump out, so someone else can jump in while you're still turning the rope.

203 **Play "Tag-Ball."** Get a tennis ball or a sponge ball. At the start of the game have everyone scatter. Try to tag someone with the ball. If you do, that person takes your place as "it," and the game starts over.

204 **Go bowling right at home.** Mark a start line and a finish line 15 feet away. Set up two soda cans 2 feet apart at the finish line. Take turns rolling the ball from the start line so it passes between the cans *without* knocking them over. If it passes through, give the player a point. If the ball goes outside the cans or a can gets knocked down, take away a point.

FRIENDLY SOLUTIONS TO FRIENDLY FIGHTS

The best thing about a fight is ending it. It's also the hardest thing about a fight sometimes. If you're too mad to think of a way out of an argument, try one of these simple solutions.

205 **Put it in writing.** Hand your angry friend a piece of gum wrapped in a piece of paper that says: "Let's start over."

206 **Draw animal footprints on a piece of paper that says: "Sorry I barked."**

207 **Flip out.** Instead of arguing about it, flip a coin to decide what you want to do.

208 **Hats off.** Write what you want to do on a piece of paper, fold it, and throw it into a hat. Have the friend you're fighting with do the same. Pick one piece of paper and do whatever it says.

209 **Play "Who's Got the Button?"** Give your friend a button, coin, pebble, or anything small to hold. Tell your friend to give his or her side of the story while holding the button. Don't interrupt. Give your side when you get the button. Keep passing the button back and forth until: a) The button wears out; b) Your hand gets sore; c) You can't remember what you were fighting about!

210 **Do activities #375, #376, and #378 (Stress**

Busters) with your friend and see if the fight blows over.

211 **Say you're hungry even if you're not.** Share your snack. Things that take a lot of chewing — bread with a hard crust, taffy, carrot sticks, caramels — work best. Talk things over when you finish eating.

212 **Find a picture of the two of you smiling.** Walk over and show it to your friend. Then think of something to do that has nothing to do with your fight.

213 **Time-out.** Hand your friend your favorite joke book or comic book. Come back in ten minutes, and your fight will probably be over.

JOIN THE CLUB!

A club adds good fun anytime. At the first meeting, choose a club name, decide on club rules, make club stuff such as membership cards, a clubhouse, club stationery, and a club treasury box, and think of things to do at your next club meeting. Here are some ideas for different kinds of clubs you can start.

214 **Organize a Detective Club.** Solve mysteries in your own home and neighborhood. Find a lost dog or locate the owner of a stray dog. Find the owner of any items you've found. Find out which delivery person has been throwing the newspaper into the bushes. Find out exactly where the ants in the kitchen are coming from. Search for buried treasure. Make mysteries of your own.

215 **Start a Pen Pal Club.** Each club member brings the name of someone he or she knows who lives in another state (cousins count!). Mix up the names and let club members pick a name out of a bag. Write letters to your club pen pals telling all about your club. Send souvenirs back and forth, such as pictures of each other, postcards from your town, and stickers.

216 **Get a Sports Club going.** Organize teams and plan regular baseball, volleyball, soccer, tennis, hockey, or basketball games.

217 **Organize a Nature Cleanup Club.** Meet once a week to clean up local sites. Pick up cans and bottles, papers and trash, and other litter. Take a walk and keep an eye out for pollution problems right in your own neighborhood — newspapers thrown out with the garbage, glass bottles and cans not recycled, paint cans or oily rags stored where there's not enough ventilation. Create a nature newsletter to make your neighbors more aware of what they can do to keep the earth clean.

218 **Set up a Movie Club.** Go to movies as a group, or rent, borrow, or share taped movies of your own or from the library. Watch them at a club meeting and discuss them like real movie critics. Serve popcorn and keep a list of the movies your club liked and didn't like. When you have a lot of movies on your list with a mini-review for each one, offer it to your local video store so they can give it to customers who may want help selecting good movies for kids.

219 **Start a Swap Club.** Each week get together for trading. Trade baseball cards, tapes, stickers, or anything else you collect. Make sure to establish a "trade-back rule." If, after three days, anyone is not happy with a trade made, the trade can be reversed.

220 **Get a Dance Club started.** Learn all the latest dances. At meetings, play music and teach each other new steps.

221 **Organize a Cheering Club.** Be the official cheer-leaders for local soccer, baseball, softball, or hockey teams that don't have a cheering squad. Make up new cheers or add dance steps to old cheers, and practice them at meetings.

222 **Start a Service Club.** Organize neighborhood food drives to collect canned goods for needy families. Do errands for elderly people who cannot get out. Learn songs to sing at local nursing homes. Provide free baby-sitting services for parents who need to run quick errands and don't want to wake the baby. Collect used toys in good condition to donate to orphanages. Collect used books to give to literacy programs. Call the local social services office to find out how you can be most helpful.

223 **Get a Lunch Bunch Club started.** Plan a weekly lunch or picnic. Each club member brings one dish to share. Plan special events for the lunches, such as an art show, a fashion show, a toy auction, or a talent show.

224 **Begin an Adventure Club.** Hold your meetings in a new and interesting outdoor place each week — up in a big tree, by a creek, in a park, or in a tent. Plan athletic contests, picnics, bike rides, or hikes. Keep a journal of your club's adventures.

225 **Start a Reading Club.** All members read the same book. At the meeting serve snacks and discuss the book. Talk about the story, the characters, and have one person find out something about the author. Write a club letter to your favorite author.

226 **Begin a Board Game Club.** Set up checkerboards, chessboards, or any other kind of game boards. Then play the games in pairs and have a championship tournament with the two winning players in the final play-off.

227 **Start a Crafts Club.** Get together to make holiday wreaths or ornaments, Halloween decorations, gifts, or things to sell. Make something different each week.

228 **Start a Computer Club.** Meet and start a desktop newspaper, design cards, write letters, or just play games.

♥ **HOME ALONE**

This is the moment you've been waiting for—to be home alone so you can do anything you want to do. But what do you want to do? Here, maybe this will help.

229 **If you live in a house, make noise.** (If you live in an apartment building, *don't!*) No one will tell you to be quiet. Scream. Play the piano loudly. Blast your favorite CD or tape. Turn the volume up on the video game system so you can really hear those explosions. Say whatever you want as loudly as you want.

230 **Make yourself a snack you always wanted but were afraid to ask for.** Every ingredient that sounds good to you is there for the taking. Make a banana split. Make a super sub sandwich. Drown a frozen waffle in ice cream, whipped cream, and chocolate sauce. Or just eat carrot sticks dipped in ranch dressing.

231 **Make your room a disaster area.** Take out your entire baseball card collection and spread it out on the floor. Leave your dirty laundry in a heap in the corner of the room. Don't make your bed. Don't hang up your clothes. Don't clear off your dresser or your desk. Be a slob.

232 **There, now start over.** Now that you've done all the "don'ts," try some "do's." Read a good book. No one will interrupt you.

233 **Watch your favorite TV show.** Your family isn't there to switch the channel as soon as you get up to go to the bathroom. Go ahead. The TV is all yours for now.

234 **Call a friend if you get lonely.**

235 **Fix something that needs fixing.** It's the perfect time to do home repairs.

236 **If you get lonely, look through family photo albums to see friendly faces.**

237 **Plan a surprise for when your family returns.** Clean your room. Organize the kitchen cabinets. Alphabetize the family CD or tape collection. Or just make a sign saying, *"Welcome Back!"* even if they were only gone for an hour.

238 **Organize your video-game collection.** Put the games in alphabetical order, or group them by category — sports, adventure, and puzzles.

239 **Find treasures right in your own house.** Lift chair and sofa cushions to find lost change. Look behind things that never get moved to find long-lost toys. Get down on the floor and look around from that lower level to find missing things. Check the "junk" drawer. You're sure to find things you never knew were there.

240 **Hide secret notes all over the house.** Simply write "Boo!" or "Gotcha!" Stick the notes in drawers, pockets, cabinets, shoes, on mirrors, in closets, anywhere your family is sure to go.

241 **Time yourself as you stand on your head.** No one else is home to distract you or knock you over.

242 **Call your parents at work.** Leave a message saying: "Have a good day. Everything is fine at home."

243 **Organize your family's map collection.** Fold all the maps correctly (this could take all day!). Then alphabetize the maps by state.

244 **Write a paper on why being home alone is not so bad.** Turn it in for your next free writing assignment.

245 **Make a rubber-band ball.** Search the whole house for every rubber band you can find. Start by making a small lump of four or five rubber bands, then add the others.

246 **Make a tape of yourself talking about what it's like to be home alone.** Tell yourself about your plans for the day. Tell your secret thoughts. You can always erase it later.

LET'S PARTY!

Celebrate anything. Celebrate nothing. Break out the confetti and P-A-R-T-Y!

247 **Organize a House-to-House Party with your neighborhood friends.** Start the party with snacks at one house. Move on to the next house for a quick dish. Dance at the house with the best music. Then wind up with dessert at your house!

248 **Invite everyone to a Backwards Party.** Write out invitations in mirrored writing. Wear clothes backwards. Don't forget to eat dessert first!

249 **Have a Come-as-You-Are Party at 7:30 A.M. on a Saturday morning.** Call up your friends at seven and tell them to be at your house in half an hour. Make it simple: juice, doughnuts, hot chocolate.

250 **Give your pet a party.** Then throw him a bone or cat treat.

251 **No pet? Give your favorite stuffed animal or doll a party.** Invite their friends *and* their owners as chaperones.

252 **Hold a Leap Year Party every four years.** Plan the party during the other three years.

253 **Have a party on the shortest day of the year, usually December 21.** Make it the shortest party ever. One drink, one food, one song, one game, then time to go home.

254 Throw a Halloween Party in the summer. Wouldn't it be nice to wear your costume without three layers of clothes underneath and a big winter coat on top?

255 Have a Crazy Hat Party. Tell all your friends to raid their families' closets and attics or poke through local rummage sales for wild headgear.

256 Organize a Make-Your-Own Crazy Hat Party. Many crafts stores sell cheap, white painters' hats. Pick up fabric paints, sequins, and colored glues for the wildest hats ever.

257 Celebrate "Parents' Day." Never heard of it? Neither have your parents, but they'll love it! Make them a card and do something nice for them.

258 Celebrate Friday afternoons with a one-hour T.G.I.F. Party right after school. D.B.Y.O.B. (*Don't* Bring Your Own Books!)

259 Cheer up a bad day with a Rotten Day Party. Wear black. Make faces. Draw your worst picture.

260 Celebrate your last day of school. Brainstorm summer plans and outings with your friends.

261 Have a Collecting Party. Invite people who have the same hobby, and trade whatever you collect.

262 When you're too busy to put on a party, let your guests do all the work. Ask each of your friends to bring one dish, one game, one tape, and to help set up and clean up.

263 Have a Midsummer's Eve Party on June 21.

Toast marshmallows over a barbecue grill to celebrate the day — the longest, lightest day of the year.

264 **Organize a House-to-House Cleanup Party on a Saturday morning.** Help each other clean up messy rooms. Have each person list three or four simple jobs that need doing. Set a timer for fifteen minutes to see who can "beat the clock." Celebrate with a pizza lunch at the last house.

265 **Hold a Mystery Guest Party.** Invite each guest to bring someone most of the guests don't know. Adults, neighbors, brothers, sisters, even pets and toys allowed, encouraged, and welcomed!

266 **Have a Swap-over Party instead of a Sleep-over.** Ask guests to bring one item to swap: a piece of clothing, a game, a book, a tape.

267 **Organize a Favorite Foods Party.** Each person brings his or her favorite food to the party then sets it out on a buffet table for all the guests to share.

☆ # NOTHING TO DO IN THIS NEIGHBORHOOD

Of all the places in the world your family had to live, they had to pick Dull Street! If your street is so boring, the squirrels go to another neighbor-hood to have fun, get busy. Turn your street into the most fun place in town!

268 **Make up a phone tree of all the kids in the neighborhood.** Use the phone tree whenever you want to organize a neighborhood activity.

269 **Find a hideout.** Every neighborhood has secret places behind bushes, in trees, or between buildings. Find one and set up neighborhood headquarters with a milk crate to sit on, a clipboard to write on, and a friend to hide out with.

270 **Keep a camouflage outfit in your closet.** Wear it for neighborhood adventures.

271 **Start Post Office Box Y.O.U.** Explore the neighborhood with your closest friends to find secret mail drops where you can leave messages for each other.

272 **Have a paper boat race on wet days.** When the gutters are flowing, get going. Call up your friends and tell them all to show up with paper boats wherever the water is rushing by the curbs.

273 **Have a neighborhood snowman contest on the first snow day of the year.** Award ribbons for the tallest, plumpest, handsomest, silliest, or most monstrous-looking snow creature.

274 **If your street has no identity, give it some.** Plant tiny alyssum seeds in the cracks of the sidewalk or near the curb. Buy a few extra packets to give to neighbors when they notice how pretty your sidewalk garden is. Pretty soon your whole street will be in bloom.

275 **Have a Beautification Day.** Sweep, dust, weed, and pick up litter in the public areas of your neighborhood.

276 **Grow one tall sunflower out front every summer.** If other people get jealous of your six-foot masterpiece, give 'em a sunflower seed to plant *next* summer.

277 **Start a pizza party tradition right before Halloween trick or treating.** Get neighborhood kids and adults to organize a simple party on your street at 4:00 P.M. Halloween afternoon. Jobs to do: Make and hand out flyers; collect money for drinks and pizza delivery; get volunteers to bring cider, napkins, a table, and a garbage can. Set up a table with cider, cups, napkins, a pizza cutter, and garbage can. Tell guests — old and young — to come in costume, or at least with a painted face or funny hat. Finish the party with a quick parade before trick or treating starts.

278 **Hold a neighborhood pet show.** Award prizes to all creatures great and small. Some categories: curliest tail, longest ears, warmest nose, scaliest skin, brightest feathers, saddest eyes. People without pets can be the judges.

279 **Chalk maze.** Draw a complicated maze on a

driveway or dead-end road. Time kids trying to get to the end.

280 **Hold a Chalk Art Show.** Have neighbors decorate their sidewalks or driveways with chalk art. Ask the "walkers" and "joggers" from the neighborhood to be the judges.

281 **Hold a giant toy fair.** Tell neighborhood kids to bring outgrown toys to display on the lawn. Give people "scrip" (fake money) to buy other toys at the fair.

282 **Be a neighborhood detective.** When you're just hanging around with your friends, try observing people who go by. See who can remember the most details about the people who pass by.

NOTHING TO DO
IN THIS TOWN

Sure there is. People all around your town are busy. Go watch the action, or make some action of your own!

283 **Play cards.** Get business cards from every local business and start a collection!

284 **Check the yellow pages.** Go through the local yellow pages to find weird or interesting local businesses and services, then go check them out.

285 **Go to the local thrift shop.** Spend a lot of time looking for something fun to buy with a dollar.

286 **Be a tourist in your own town.** Visit a local site. Ask the people there to recommend places to eat or things to see and do in your town. Then do them. Don't forget to buy a postcard!

287 **Be kind to animals.** Go around the neighborhood and collect old towels and blankets. Take them to the local animal shelter.

288 **Go back in time.** Go to the local historical society or the public library and see how your town looked a long time ago. Stop in all the antique shops to see what kids a long time ago did when *they* were bored!

289 **Build up.** Pass the time watching any local construction that's taking place. How *do* they pave around those manhole covers anyway?

290 **Be classy.** Find out if you can visit local karate, dance, cooking, art, music, or drama classes.

291 **Take a walk in the local cemetery.** It's free, and you know it'll be quiet! Look for the oldest and newest stones. Read the inscriptions and try to imagine what the deceased persons were like.

292 **See what your town is like after hours.** Ask your parents to take you on a special town tour in the middle of the night!

NOTHING TO DO ON THIS PLANET!

Nonsense! Here are just some of the things you can do for this planet.

293 **Have a recycling art show.** Make sculptures, collages, and other works of art using materials that might otherwise have been thrown out. Advertise your art show on posters made of used grocery bags. Display your art outdoors in front of your house or apartment building.

294 **Collect seedpods from trees and grow them in small pots.**

295 **Celebrate special occasions by planting a tree.** Instead of buying birthday presents, plant a birthday tree, a Mother's or Father's Day Tree, and any other special trees during the planting season.

296 **Make a reusable lunch bag.** Use canvas or any heavy material. Cut out a bag shape using a paper lunch bag as your pattern. Sew up the sides. Use fabric markers to decorate and write your name on the bag.

297 **Organize stream-cleaning parties.** If you live near a stream, get a group of neighbors together with rakes, trash bags, and fishnets. Wear high rubber boots and walk through the stream picking up litter that's been thrown in. Use the nets to skim off other floating debris.

298 **Make a litterbag for your car.** Decorate a lunch bag. Staple a strip of paper onto the bag to use as a handle. Hang the bag over a door handle or radio knob.

299 **Make a Save-the-Planet Idea Chart for your house.** Include such ideas as turning off water while dishwashing or teeth-brushing; fixing leaky faucets; biking or walking short distances instead of driving; using rags instead of paper towels; using both sides of writing or drawing paper. Leave space on the chart for other family members to add good ideas.

300 **Plan a Litter Hunt.** Give each hunter a bag for collecting litter. The person who fills the bag the fullest wins the hunt. (Hide a treasure treat along the route, such as peanuts in their shells or wrapped candies, so the hunters find something good to eat, too!)

301 **Stack and bundle newspapers for the recycling center.**

302 **Start a Planet-Saver Kids' Club.**

303 **Have a Planet-Saver Contest at home.** Have everyone in your house make a list of things you can all do to help keep the environment clean.

304 **Take a survey of businesses in your area.** Find out which store or business is doing the most for the environment. Make a poster for the winning business to display. The poster might say: *"The Planet-Saver Kids' Club awards this poster to this store for outstanding attention to the conservation of our planet."*

♥ WHO'S NEW? YOU!

Oh, no. The new kid is you! At school. At camp. In the neighborhood. On the team. Anywhere that you're the newcomer, try out these easy icebreakers.

305 **Wear your name.** For the first couple of weeks in a new place, wear or carry around whatever personalized things you have. This will help kids, teachers, and counselors learn your name fast.

306 **Repeat new names as soon as you're introduced.** Use a new person's name right away to help remember it. When you're first introduced say "Hi, Matt," or "Hi, Erin." Then try to use that person's name once or twice again when you start talking.

307 **Be an extra!** Extra prepared, that is. Somebody always shows up at new places without all the right stuff — pens, stamps, tissues, paper, markers, flashlights, books. With extra supplies on hand to lend, you'll make friends right away.

308 Don't leave home without it. Without what? Something to do while teachers, counselors, and coaches get organized. Stash pocket games, cards, or even a cat's cradle string in your pocket for slow times wherever you go.

309 Ask for directions even if you're not lost.

310 Ask what time it is even if you're wearing a watch.

311 Bring along a friendship bracelet string board to new places. In no time someone will look over your shoulder to admire your talent. Hand the person the bracelet when you're done, and start a new friendship!

312 Carry around the latest PRESIDENT MEETS SPACE ALIEN tabloid newspaper. Somebody's sure to ask you for a peek.

313 Don't just stand there, *do* something. If you're shy and can't make the first move to meet people, let your actions bring people to you. Sit with a sketch pad and draw what you see in your new neighborhood. Walk around with a camera and take pictures. Or just bounce a tennis ball on the strings of your racket until you break your own record. Somebody is bound to ask you about what you're doing.

314 Learn three simple magic tricks and share them with people.

315 Have a few good jokes on hand to share.

316 Carry around a pack of optical illusion cards.

Look at them when other kids are around. They won't be able to resist a peek.

317 **Learn "Heart and Soul" even if you don't play the piano.**

318 **Take along a joke book.** Put it where other kids can see it. Lend it out. Know where to find the best jokes.

319 **Be a Good-for-Something.** Whatever you're good at is good for getting you in good with everyone. Volunteer to help someone with homework, baseball batting practice, a science fair project, or whatever your talent-to-spare might be.

320 **Have a Meet-the-New-Kid-Party in your own honor.** Invite the whole class or group to an outdoor celebration. Play softball, volleyball, touch football, or just have an old-fashioned three-legged race.

321 **Tell fortunes.** The first day at camp doesn't have to be the worst day at camp. Get off to a great start with your bunkmates by "reading fortunes." Look at each new friend's palm and deliver all the good news. There's a new friend in their future — you! (Add some other good stuff, too, such as, "You'll be great at anything you do. Good health, lots of money, and a great camp experience are all in your future!")

322 **Be a good neighbor.** When you move to a new neighborhood, make yourself useful. Offer to rake leaves, weed gardens, carry newspapers to the door (then to the curb on recycling day), carry in recycling bins and trash cans, or help out in any way you can. Some of the neighbors probably have kids your age.

323 **Organize a Moving-In Sale.** Have the tag sale you didn't have time for at your old house. You'll make new friends *and* money.

✂ SICK OF BEING HOMESICK

Whether you're away at camp, visiting a faraway relative, or just sleeping over at a new friend's house, missing home can make you miss out on all the fun. Try these quick fixes for homesickness.

324 **Take a picture of your mom and dad.** Think about how much they miss you. Now think of what you could say to them right now to help them get through their first lonely night without you.

325 **Write a letter to yourself.** Tell yourself all the reasons you should be glad to be away from home right now.

326 **Keep a survival journal.** Each day that you are away, write about how you made it through another day. Write down your bad or sad feelings, then write about what you did to make yourself feel better.

327 **Find someone who feels worse than you do.** Take your mind off your own worries by helping that person get over the rough spots.

328 **Fill in this blank with the name of any food you hate:** _____
Aren't you glad you're not home eating that?

329 **Make a list of your chores at home.** Post your list where you'll see it a lot. Isn't it great nobody can make you do these chores while you're away?

☆ SICK OF BEING SICK

What can you do to take the boredom out of sick days? You guessed it! Read this list!

330 **Make yourself a Get Well pillowcase with fabric markers.**

331 **How about a "Get Well" sleep shirt?** Ask for a nice, old, soft T-shirt from Dad or an older brother. Decorate it with fabric markers to match your pillow.

332 **Make a funny sign for the sickroom door.** "Enter at Your Own Risk" or "Leave Gifts on Table Next to Bed."

333 **Make a homemade guest book.** Have visitors sign in then write or draw something cheery.

334 **Treat your nose to some monogrammed tissues.** Using a pen, write your initials on each tissue in a pack. Use them when people come to wish you well.

335 **Soften up your tissues.** If your nose is red and sore, dab a few drops of baby oil in each of your tissues. This will help your nose heal.

336 **Make friendly ghosts.** Ball up one tissue. Cover it with another one. Fasten the "head" with a rubber band. Keep these ghosties in a basket by your bed for spooky company.

337 **Fix your hair different ways every day you're sick in bed.** It'll get out the tangles, and you'll feel better, too, when at least one part of you looks good.

338 **Make a list of the best things about being sick.** Tape it to the headboard.

339 **Make a list of the worst things about being sick.** Bunch it up and throw it in the wastebasket.

340 **Watch a television show without the sound on.** Make up your own story.

341 **Make a Get Well card for yourself.**

342 **Make flavored ice cubes.** Use orange juice or other fruit juice and suck on the cubes if you have a sore throat.

343 **Count spots.** Count your spots every day if you have a rash, chicken pox, or measles. When the number goes down, you're on the mend!

344 **Mix up a rash-soother recipe.** Mix baking soda

and lemon juice into a paste. Spread it over the itchiest part of your body and let it dry.

345 **Invent a cure for your own cold.** Create a drink that tastes delicious. (Just making it yourself will help!)

346 **Make a Sick-of-Being-Sick Scorecard.** Keep a running count of coughs, sneezes, and number of tissues used.

347 **Read funny books.** Learn a new joke each day you are sick.

348 **Have a contest for visitors.** Fill a big jar with jelly beans or M & M's. Only you know how many are in the jar. Let each visitor fill out a slip of paper with his or her name and the number guessed. When you are well again, give the winner the whole jar.

349 **Take a bubble bath.** Blow bubbles in the tub. Bubbles always cheer up sick people.

350 **Act healthy.** Get up, brush your teeth, wash your face, get dressed, eat a good breakfast. See if acting well really makes you well. If it doesn't, go back to bed.

351 **Put on a happy face.** Just because you don't feel good doesn't mean you can't look good. Add color to your pale cheeks with your mother's makeup. And while you're at it, add a clown-sized smile, freckles across your nose, and anything else that makes your face happy.

352 **Do the crossword puzzle in the daily newspaper.**

If it's too hard, make up your own puzzle — fill in the squares and try to make your own words fit together.

353 **Color in the daily comics.**

354 **Have someone take pictures of you every day.** Get shots of you lying in bed, blowing your nose, sleeping, having visitors. Make a photo album and call it, "The Sick-of-Being-Sick Picture Album."

 # GROUNDED!

When you hear, "Go to your room!" that's when you need things to do. You may not be allowed out of your room, but that's no reason to go out of your mind with boredom!

355 **Write out your version of what got you in hot water.** Add an apology at the end even if you're sure you're right. Slip it under the door of your room so your parents will find it.

356 **Make up a sad song about how sorry you are.** Sing it to your parents without cracking a smile.

357 **Draw an ugly picture of the person who sent you to your room.** Tear it into a zillion pieces. Drop the pieces one by one into the wastebasket. There — now don't you feel better?

358 **Mirror art.** Sit in front of a mirror with a pencil and paper. Try to draw what you see in the reflection without looking down.

359 **Organize your sock drawer.**

360 **Do some of the Stress Busters (#373–#388).**

361 **Work out.** Do jumping jacks, deep knee-bends, toe-touches, sit-ups, leg-lifts, and push-ups.

362 **Think.** If you're not allowed to even get off your bed, do math problems in your head.

363 **Count until you're allowed to come out of your room.** See how high you can go.

364 **Take a nap.** Maybe you got in trouble because you were overtired.

365 **Put on a funny face.** Stand in front of the mirror and make faces at yourself. Pretty soon you'll be laughing.

CHANGE A NO TO A YES

Don't take no for an answer. Change it to a yes! When you want permission or a favor, and the head-shaking starts, turn on the smiles and these ideas before you give up.

366 **Start every request with: "Could you think about whether . . . ?"** It's easier for someone to say yes to *thinking* about something than to say yes right away. While the person is thinking, do some of the following activities to improve your chances for a yes.

367 **Put it in writing.** Write your request and the reasons it should be granted in a note — or a lot of little notes tucked in places around the house where your parents will see them.

368 **Picket.** Make a sign with your request. Tape it to a broomstick and march around the house until your parents are laughing so hard they accidentally say yes to what you want!

369 **Draw some "Pretty Pleases."** Design some tiny notes that say "Pretty Please" on the front in pretty letters. Inside write a good reason you should get your request.

370 **Don't ask it, sing it.** Make up a silly song asking for the favor.

371 **Wish upon a star.** Cut a star out of gray or yellow construction paper. Put three wishes on it — two funny ones and your real wish. Put the star where your parents will find it.

372 **Trade ya.** See if you can make a swap. If you play your friend's favorite game now, then she'll play your game later. Swap chores with your brother. Or empty the dishwasher in exchange for extra dessert.

It's no fair! You have tons of homework. Your little brother started a fight, and you got blamed. Your best friend just went off someplace without you. Here are some ways to let off steam.

373 **Blow up a bunch of balloons and make a balloon bouquet for your room.** Believe it or not, all that inhaling and exhaling will relieve stress, and the balloon bouquet will make you feel better.

374 **Make a Velcro target for your room.** Attach a big piece of Velcro to your wall or bulletin board. Aim a sponge ball at the Velcro. Keep throwing until you feel better.

375 **Take it out on paper.** Keep a stack of all kinds of scrap paper in a "Stress" pile in your room. When you feel tense, scrunch, bunch, rip, and tear away at the paper. You can use the paper over and over for this activity.

376 **Bag it!** Inflate some extra plastic or paper bags and pop them.

377 **Whomp it!** Punch your pillow, or a beanbag chair if you have one.

378 **Bounce your bad feelings away.** Get a basketball and bounce it a hundred times on a sidewalk or driveway.

379 **Make believe you have no bones.** Sit cross-legged or lie on the floor. Then, toe to head, tell each part of your body to relax, toe by toe, foot by foot, leg by leg, etc.

380 Listen up. Lie down on your bed. Close your eyes. Concentrate on every sound — the clock ticking, a bird outside, cars honking, voices in other rooms. Listen hard for at least five minutes.

381 Freeze and melt. No, don't open the refrigerator. Go to your room. Lie down on your bed or the floor. Tighten your toes, feet, and legs and "freeze" them. Then slowly "thaw" them out by relaxing each muscle one by one. Do the same with your fingers, hands, arms, stomach, head, neck, and back.

382 Focus. Put something small on the wall — a pin, a flower, a sticker. Stare at it as long as you can.

383 Let the eyes have it. Face a wall in your room. Sit cross-legged in front of it. Make your eyes sweep up and down 10 times, then sideways 10 times, then diagonally 10 times. Come back to the middle each time.

384 Go ballooning. Pretend your lungs are a collapsed balloon. Slowly fill up your "balloon" by breathing in deeply. Now slowly exhale, and let your balloon slowly collapse again. Do this 10 times.

385 Shake it all around. Shake the stress away. Stand in the middle of your room. Think of a freezing cold day or the way you feel when you come out of cold water. Shake yourself all over. Then lie down on your bed and pretend you're drying yourself off on a sunny, hot beach.

386 **Be your own fan.** Stand up with your feet wide apart and your arms dangling. Then lift your arms to shoulder height and pretend you are a ceiling fan slow-fanning everything below you. Now reverse and turn the "fan" on in the other direction.

387 **Bridge over troubled waters.** Lie flat on the floor. Slowly arch your back up from the floor then slowly lower it. Do this three or four times until all those tight kinks you were feeling are gone.

388 **String yourself along.** Cut a five-foot section of string. Put it in a circle on the grass. Sit inside the circle. Concentrate on everything you see inside the circle for five minutes.

MORE THINGS TO DO ON YOUR OWN

Have a little fun all by yourself.

389 **Play "As the Ceiling Turns."** Put your arms out and turn around and around and around about ten times. Lie flat on your back on the floor and look up at the ceiling. You stopped turning, but the ceiling didn't!

390 **Go outside and look for four-leaf clovers.**

391 **Make a handprint to keep.** Spread a thin layer of white glue evenly over one hand — from fingertips to the edge of your wrist. Wait for it to dry completely. Carefully peel it off. You'll have a perfect handprint showing every line.

392 **Test the U.S. mail.** Write a letter to yourself and mail it to yourself. See how long it takes to reach you. See how long it takes you to write back!

393 **Try cracker whistling.** Chew a mouthful of crumbled saltine crackers. While they are still dry and before you swallow, try whistling.

394 **Build a pillow fort and hide in it.**

395 **Call all your friends and do a survey.** Ask them what they're wearing or what they're doing. Find out how many of them are bored right now. Then invite them over and do #184–#204.

396 **Search for silver.** Empty your cash box or piggy bank and look through all your dimes and quarters. Any that are dated earlier than 1965 are valuable because they have more silver in them than the new coins.

397 **Count to see if you still have eleven fingers.** Start on one hand, counting backward — 10, 9,

8, 7, 6. Add the other five, and you've got 11! Don't ask, just do it.

398 **Read one whole page of the newspaper and look for mistakes.** Look for spelling errors, words repeated twice, and wrong captions under pictures. Circle the mistakes in red, and send it to the Editor's Desk of the newspaper. Hint: The early edition usually has more mistakes.

399 **Listen to a sports event on the radio.**

400 **Play paper basketball.** Make a paper ball. Practice shooting into an empty wastebasket.

401 **Start a phone wave.** Call a friend and tell him or her to catch the wave by calling another friend to do the same thing. See how long it takes for "the wave" to catch you back.

402 **Change the way your shoes are laced up.** Use two different-colored laces. Lace from top to bottom. Lace crisscross. Lace vertically without crossing. Invent a new lacing style of your own.

403 **See the world upside down.** Tape a small mirror to the center of a notebook or magazine cover. Hold the book against your chest. Tilt it so that you can see the ceiling in the mirror, but not your face. Walk as you look in the mirror. Pretty soon, you'll be stepping over things! It's an optical illusion and fun to try!

404 **Find some empty boxes.** Make something out of them. A submarine. A pet carrier. Anything.

405 **Plan a dream vacation.** Write down where you would go, what you would do, whom you would bring along, what would make it the best vacation ever!

406 **Make up a new holiday for the month of August.** August is the only month with no holidays.

☆ COMMERCIAL-BREAK GAMES

When commercial breaks take longer than the show, boredom is bound to set in. Here are some games to play with advertisers.

407 **Write down the name of the product being advertised.** See how many words you can make out of the letters in the name before the show comes back on.

408 **Count how many times the announcer says "new" in the commercial.**

409 **Run up and down the stairs during commercials.** Keep track of your scores to see which programs run the longest commercials.

410 **Count how many adjectives the announcer uses to describe the product.** Listen for words like "great," "fantastic," "amazing."

411 **Turn down the sound.** Make up your own words to sell the product. Make up a silly commercial that is sure *not* to sell the product!

412 Count how many red-haired actors and actresses appear in commercials.

413 Count how many kid actors are in commercials.

414 Count how many commercials make men look stupid.

415 Count how many commercials make women look stupid.

416 Count how many pet food commercials make cats or dogs look human.

417 Count how many pet food commercials make cats or dogs look stupid.

418 Keep track of how many commercials are funny.

419 Keep track of how many commercials *try* to be funny but aren't.

420 Count how many commercials are serious.

421 Keep track of how many commercials use songs to sell a product.

422 Play "Name That Commercial Tune" during commercials. Turn off the sound during breaks. Have viewers each take turns singing one or two notes of commercial songs to see who can guess the tune and the product it advertises.

AFTER DINNER, BEFORE BED

Hurry! It's not quite bedtime yet. You still have just enough time to have some fun. Here's how!

423 **Get to know the shadow creatures in your room.** Turn off the lights and find the shadows. Turn on the lights and find the objects that created the shadows.

424 **Take a shower and change your hairstyle.** While your hair is wet, style it in all different ways. Brush it up, brush it down, brush it all over.

425 **Arrange every stuffed animal in the house around the walls of your room.** Think of them as "roommates" for the night.

426 **Take a walk before bed.** Whether it's summer, winter, spring, or fall, a walk after dinner helps your stomach get settled so the rest of your body can get settled, too. Count the stars, fireflies, bats, or birds flying to their night spots, or just count the steps you take.

427 **Listen to the radio instead of watching television.** Find out what's on at this time of night.

428 **Don't read a bedtime book.** Write or dictate a story into a tape recorder. Play it back before bed on another night.

429 Ask someone in your house to read *you* a story.

430 Do some Stress Busters (#373–#388) to wind down.

431 Play "Flashlight Tag" in the dark with other kids.

432 Play "Spotlight." Give the "It" person a flashlight. Tell "It" to sit in the middle of the yard or room with eyes shut. Line the other players in front of "It." Players have to sneak by as silently as possible. When "It" hears someone, he or she points the flashlight at the player. If the player is caught in the light, that person becomes "It" for the next round. Keep playing until it's time to go in.

433 Paste glow-in-the-dark star decals on your ceiling. Before you get into bed, flash a flashlight on the "stars." When you turn off the lights, the stars will be brighter than usual.

LIGHTS OUT, CAN'T SLEEP

Before your eyes close for the night, try some of these bright night ideas.

434 Say the alphabet in your head. Say it backward. Keep saying it until you fall asleep.

435 Plan your dream for the night. Lie in bed and

think of all the things you would love to dream about. Fall asleep and dream.

436 Don't move a muscle. Lie as still as you can.

437 Close your eyes and pretend you're sunbathing. Imagine you're on a beautiful beach. Breathe in deeply and think of the sound of the waves washing in and out on the shore.

438 Watch the moon. If you can see it from your window, stare at it and see how long it takes to move out of your view.

439 Chant. Find one word you like to say, a soothing word such as "hum." Say it over and over and over in your head.

440 Plan a perfect day in your head. Think of all your favorite people, activities, music, food, and places. Plan a day when you get to see, try, or visit all your favorites.

441 Go back in time. Pick a perfect day you already had and try to remember every detail of it.

442 Sleep in another part of the house. Take your sleeping bag and a pillow and camp out someplace other than your bedroom.

443 Try "Ways to Do Nothing When There's Nothing to Do" (#992–#1,001).

444 Try on different pajamas. Maybe the ones you have on are too thin or picky or twisty.

445 Guess objects in the darkness. Sweep things off your dresser and desk onto your bed. See if you can guess what they are in the darkness before you put them back.

446 **Play some soft music.** If you still have a tape of children's lullabies from when you were little, try playing that.

447 **Sing lullabies.** Make up the words you can't remember. Just the tune might be enough to make you fall asleep.

448 **Keep glow-in-the-dark stuff by your bed.** Fiddle with this stuff when you can't sleep.

❤ UP TOO EARLY, AND NO ONE ELSE IS AWAKE YET

Boredom can strike at any hour — even in the early morning. Here's just the help you need.

449 **Call in a song request to your favorite radio station.** You'll have a good chance of getting through. Then pass the time listening for your song to be played.

450 **Be an early-morning birdbrain.** Listen to the birds. They're up early, too. Tape record their morning songs.

451 **Make static electricity sparks with your acrylic blanket.** In the early morning darkness it will be easy to see the tiny flashes of light under your covers if you flap them up and down quickly.

452 **Don't get up yet.** Just lie in bed and find a spot on the wall. Stare at it until it moves.

453 **Rearrange the furniture in your room without moving a thing.** Redecorate your room in your head. Try to picture the best arrangement. Maybe even rearrange your room later on.

454 **Make up a wake-up song for yourself.**

455 **Get up and invent a Super Secret Breakfast.** Turn plain toast into "Toast of the Town." Spread peanut butter on it, add honey and shredded coconut.

456 **Count mice, not sheep.** Watch early morning cartoons and count how many mice are in all the cartoons combined.

457 **Find your best smile.** Now's the perfect time to brush your teeth, floss them, and flash them at your own reflection in the bathroom mirror. Practice big smiles, half-smiles, closed-mouth smiles, and a smile from every angle. See which one pleases you the most. Use it often.

458 **Write "Good Morning!" notes to everyone else in the family.** Place the notes on the sleeping people's pillows, tape them to the bathroom mirror, or on each person's favorite box of cereal.

459 **Write "Good Morning!" on the bathroom mirror with soap.**

460 **Make your bed while you're still in it.** Pull all the covers and the spread up to your chin, then slowly and carefully slide out. Fluff your pillow and pull the spread over it.

461 **Send mental messages to your best friend.** Stay in bed and lie very still. Think of a message you'd like to send — something as simple as: "Call me as soon as you wake up." Concentrate very, very hard and imagine your message traveling from your mind to your friend's mind. If your friend calls, ask what made him or her think to call.

462 **Pretend you're a grown-up waking up very early.** Quietly get up, go outside, get the newspaper, pour yourself some orange juice in a coffee mug, then sit at the table and read the paper while you drink from the mug. If you don't really like it, be a kid again.

463 **Learn how to say "Good Morning" in a few languages.** *Bonjour! Buon giorno! Buenos días!*

464 **Learn a few French words while everyone is sleeping.** When everyone gets up pretend you became a French person in the night and only speak French to them. Practice: *Bonjour* (bone-*jure*); *Parlez-vous français?* (*Par*-lay-voo-fraun-*say*); *merci* (mare-*see*); *oui* (we); and *non* (no).

465 **Spin a web.** If you have a sister or brother, make a thread web around the sleeper's bed. Tie one end to a bedpost and weave the thread back and forth around the room. What a surprise!

466 **Put a fake sleeping body in your bed.** Go hide in your closet to watch and listen when someone tries to wake "you." A couple of pillows under the blanket should do the trick!

467 **Think.** When you're lying in bed and you think you're doing nothing, you're actually doing a lot. In fact your brain is sending and receiving 100,000 messages per second! (Who was ever able to count that fast?!)

468 **Measure yourself as soon as you get up.** Write down your morning height so you can compare it to your night height. You'll find that you are a little bit taller in the morning than at night because after lying down all night, your backbone is stretched to its full length!

469 **If it's very, very early, watch the sun rise.** See how long it takes to come up all the way.

 # STORMY NIGHTS, NO LIGHTS

You can stand the thunder. You can stand the lightning. But can you stand it when the electricity goes out? Sure you can!

470 **Make a "silent movie" with your flashlight.** One person shines the light on another, moving the light back and forth as fast as possible. The moving person can go fast or slow, moving hands, fingers, the whole body, or just facial features. The look is the same as in old, silent movies.

471 **Make a flashlight story circle.** Set up a flashlight on the floor and sit in a circle around it. Tell stormy-night ghost stories or other scary tales.

472 **Save flashlight batteries.** Get everyone in the family to sleep in the same room. Sleeping bags make even the stormiest nights feel cozy, safe, and warm.

473 **Make a stormy-night supper.** Sandwiches, cereal, crackers and cheese, anything that doesn't need to be cooked. Eat it by candlelight and see how good food tastes under "crisis" conditions.

474 **Tell a book.** No reading light? Have each person tell the plot of a favorite book. Start with the title, the author, then the story.

475 **Play hand shadows.** One person points the light to the wall while another person makes shapes with two hands. Watch the wall for rabbits, wolves, birds, and other shadow creatures.

476 **Show off your X-ray vision.** Look right through your hand when you hold your fingers right over the flashlight head. You can almost see bones!

477 **Tape the thunder.** Use your battery-powered tape recorder to record the sounds of the storm. Use the tape on Halloween or any time you feel like raising a storm of your own.

478 **Keep your pet company under the bed.** Your pet will feel better.

479 Tell a never-ending stormy night story. It was a dark, dark, stormy night, on a high, high hill. There were ten men sitting around a campfire. One said, "Jack, tell us a story!" So Jack began: "It was a dark, dark, stormy night, on a high, high hill. There were ten men sitting around a camp fire. One said, 'Jack, tell us a story!' So Jack began . . ." and so on. Tell the story until someone screams in agony . . . or the lights come on.

480 Crack an egg on someone's head. No, not really. But try this trick which really feels like you did crack an egg. Make a fist with one hand and hold it lightly on someone's head. Smack your fist with your other hand. Lightly and slowly, spread your fingers on the victim's head and drip your fingers down over the hair. It feels icky, and in the stormy darkness, it should feel even ickier!

481 Guess what time the electricity will come back on. Each person makes one guess. Write all the guesses down. When the lights come back on, see who was closest to the correct time.

482 See whom you can fool. After the power has been off for a while, ask your sister or brother to turn on the TV or the kitchen light. Ask Mom if you can have a piece of toast with butter and jam. Ask Dad to turn the diswasher on. Ask everybody to do something that uses electricity. See how many of them you can catch.

483 **Play "Boom! Boom!"** Celebrate the booming of thunder with this silly game. One person says, "Boom!" The next person says, "Boom! Boom!" The next says, "Boom! Boom! Boom!" Add another "Boom!" with each turn and see if you can out-Boom the booms of thunder.

484 **Be scared silly.** If you're with friends when the lights go out, don't be afraid. Start telling the scariest story ever told. Each person adds two scary sentences to the story until you reach the end. Everyone should talk very softly and mysteriously. Make sure *you* get to finish the story. When it's time say: ". . . and as the storm roared around the frightened group only one thing, one single thing, could be heard above the thunder. That one thing was YOU SCREAMING!" Grab the person next to you when you say the last two words, and you surely will hear screams from everyone (followed by laughter, of course)!

485 **Play "Guess What's Gone?"** In the darkness you have only your hands to help you figure out what certain objects are. Take turns placing objects on a tray while the other person tries to guess which one thing has been removed. Some objects to use are: a key, a crayon, a paper clip, a barrette, a button, a ring, a coin, a lipstick.

486 **Notice who's on first?** When the electricity comes back on see how long it is before someone in the house turns on the television. What is the first electrical appliance used? What was most missed?

☆ **YOUR WALLET'S EMPTY, AND EVERYBODY'S GOING TO THE MOVIES**

Be an odd-jobber — make money doing quick jobs grown-ups hate doing.

487 Clean someone's closet.

488 Organize someone's junk drawer.

489 Alphabetize spice racks.

490 Sand and oil the garden and toolbox tools.

491 Put family photos into albums. You'll probably get double the fee for this job!

492 Organize photo negatives into labeled envelopes. Triple pay for this!

493 Cut and tape recipes onto index cards. Every cook with a folder full of yellow newspaper clippings will hire you!

494 Redeem cans and bottles for people. Take a percentage of all those nickels.

495 Polish silver.

496 Offer a door-to-door toy cleaning service.

497 Weed a garden.

498 Polish all the doorknobs in a house.

499 Vacuum lamp shades.

500 Alphabetize bookshelves.

501 Clean your little sister's or brother's room.

502 Organize the bureau drawers.

503 Clean all the switch plates in the house.

YOU LIKE TODDLERS, BUT YOU'RE TOO YOUNG TO BABY-SIT ALONE

Not to worry. Every parent needs an in-house helper for small stretches of time. Offer to entertain a toddler so busy parents can peel potatoes, take a shower, or make phone calls while you're there keeping a little one happy and busy. In a year or two, you'll be well-trained for solo baby-sitting.

504 **Be a dinner-hour storyteller.** Take your own baby books and read them out loud while parents get dinner ready.

505 **Be a movie mate.** Check out kiddie videos from the library and watch them with your small friends so their moms and dads can have a little free time right in their own houses.

506 **Take a toddler for a walk nearby.** Go to your house and show off your room. Walk to the mailbox. Ask the child to help you look for squirrels or birds.

507 **Organize a teddy bear picnic.** Make a few peanut butter sandwiches. Take along some apple juice. Don't forget your own teddy bears and a blanket and a small chair. Pass an hour or so with a toddler, setting up the picnic and then enjoying it with his or her teddy bears.

508 **Play "Fetch" instead of "Catch."** Toddlers can't always catch, but they sure love to fetch and bring you back the ball. A sponge ball works best.

509 **Make a tunnel out of a big cardboard box.** Have the toddler chase you through the box, then switch.

510 **Water, water everywhere, and none of it to drink.** Set up playtime in the bathroom sink. Take over squirt bottles, plastic cups, and small pails. You'll have buckets of fun.

511 **Shake a finger.** Draw a smiley face on your index finger and on the toddler's finger. Have the "finger puppets" talk to each other.

512 **Go grocery shopping with a toddler's parent.** Entertain the child in one shopping cart while the parent goes through the store with another one.

513 **Take over a busy bag of your old toys.**

514 **Make jewelry.** Take shoelaces and Cheerios, and make edible jewelry.

515 **Go collecting.** Go on a collecting walk for seeds and pebbles. Afterwards, glue what you collect onto construction paper.

516 **Blow bubbles.** Especially good for windy days.

517 **Paint the town.** Bring out a small pail of water and some watercolor paints, and paint pictures on the driveway or sidewalk.

518 **Play tent.** Set up a cozy area under a table by covering it with a big blanket. Bring in toys, a flashlight, and a blanket.

519 **Play dress-up with old clothes from your own house.**

520 **Have a toy wash.** Set up a dishpan of suds outside and help your little friend wash and scrub toys. Set them out to dry on the lawn.

MUST RAISE CASH FOR HOLIDAY SHOPPING

Is your gift list getting longer at the same time your wallet is getting thinner? Raise holiday present money by doing pre-holiday jobs for a fee.

521 **Address and stamp holiday card envelopes.**

522 **Wrap presents.**

523 **Be a mail carrier.** If the post office is nearby and you can walk there by yourself, offer to drop off packages, mail cards, and pick up stamps.

524 **Run errands.** If you're a good runner, charge by the errand instead of by the hour.

525 **Be a card or at least make a card.** Design custom-made holiday cards for grandparents, aunts, uncles, and special friends.

526 **Make dough while you're making dough.** Sell rolls of frozen holiday cookie dough you make. Tape on instructions for baking.

527 **Take orders for holiday treats.** A few weeks before a holiday, make a sample of cookies, cakes, fudge, or some other holiday treat. Take orders to be delivered right around the holiday. Be sure to charge enough to cover the cost of supplies and make a profit, too.

528 **Shovel snow.**

529 **Start an ice-scraping service.** Busy working people just hate scraping ice off their windshields every morning. If you're an early bird, do this annoying chore every day.

♥ ## THE BEST GIFTS IN LIFE ARE FREE

Out of cash but still have family presents to get for birthdays and other holidays? Spend time, not money, on these personalized presents.

530 **Be a helper for the day.**

531 **Give a book of coupons for future services.**

Make your sister's bed. Do your brother's chores. Vacuum the family car.

532 **Write a birthday poem.** Recite it when you serve the lucky recipient breakfast in bed.

533 **Write a mirror message with soap for the first birthday greeting of the day.**

534 **End someone's birthday with a handmade birthday card on his or her pillow.**

535 **Write "Happy Birthday" backward on poster board.** Tape it to the mirror for the birthday person to translate.

536 **Hide small homemade birthday cards all over.** Tuck birthday cards in a shoe, a sleeve, a hairbrush for daylong birthday wishes.

537 **Give the birthday person a hand or two.** Write "Happy" on one hand and "Birthday" on the other. Hold up your hands as you sing the birthday song.

538 **Say it with pictures.** Cut out big letters spelling "Happy Birthday." Have a friend take photos of you holding each letter. Develop the film and give the pictures as a present.

539 **Write "Happy Birthday" in chalk on the driveway or sidewalk.**

540 **Cut out "Happy Birthday" letters and put them in an envelope.**

541 **Buy a present and stop feeling guilty.** Read #521–#529 and #556–#572 and learn how to make quick cash.

542 **Be a coffeemaker.** Get up early and get coffee started, then deliver it to sleepy parents.

543 **Fetch the paper.**

544 **Sort laundry and put it away.** Yes, it's a drag. That's why this is such a great present to give to someone who usually does the job.

545 **Be the salad maker.** Wash, dry, and shred the lettuce, then toss it with dressing. Any cook can use a salad helper.

546 **Carry in the groceries.** Even people who don't mind shopping hate this. That's what makes this a super present.

547 **Put the groceries away.** Even better than #546.

✂ BEST FRIENDS — MUST RAISE CASH TOGETHER

You and your buddy are both broke, and a big school trip is coming up. Here are some jobs where two heads will put you ahead.

548 **Be a party pair.** Help serve food and clean up at parties.

549 **Entertain the kiddie guests at adult parties.**

550 **Act up at kiddie parties.** Get out your old puppets and create a ten-minute puppet show for children's birthday parties.

551 **Believe in magic.** Learn some magic tricks and perform them for a few minutes at a children's birthday party.

552 **Paint little faces at birthday parties.**

553 **Do some of the cousin games (#583, #585, #586, #591) for pay at children's parties.**

554 **Start a local "gofer" service.** Go for stamps, groceries, dog walks, kid walks.

555 **Rise and shine on Saturdays and Sundays.** Deliver doughnuts, newspapers, or bagels to the front door so people can stay in their pj's till noon.

☆ # NO MONEY FOR SUMMER VACATION

How did summer get here so fast? Where are you going to get money to spend over your vacation? Well, what are you waiting for? There's work to be done!

556 **Make summer holiday desserts.** Go around your neighborhood and take orders for Fourth of July or Labor Day cupcakes. Lots of people will be going to cookouts and will need to bring dessert. Take around a sample with red, white, and blue icing for the Fourth or chocolate frosting and yellow and orange sprinkles for Labor Day.

557 **Advertise a camp-clothes labeling service the day school gets out.** Sew, iron, or use laundry markers to label campers' clothes.

558 **Design thank-you cards and sell them door-to-door.**

559 **Make up one camp kit.** Fill it with cute stationery, checklist letters, stamps, treats, etc. Show it to parents of campers and take orders to make up kits to be delivered by a certain date.

560 **Build a traveling cookie or lemonade stand.** Take it to construction sites, baseball games, or a bus stop on a hot day.

561 **Have a traveling sneaker-cleaning business.** Load up a wagon with white sneaker polish and a buffing cloth. Charge per pair.

562 **Be a ball girl or ball boy at the local tennis court.** While people play tennis, you retrieve the balls they hit out of the courts. Charge by the hour.

563 **Hold a Pet Wash.**

564 **Announce Friendship Day in heart-shaped flyers.** Make and sell friendship bracelets for friends to give each other.

565 **Sell ice water to joggers.** You'd be surprised at how many hot and sweaty people will give you a nickel for a cup of plain ice water, which costs you no more than the cup!

HAVE A LITTLE MONEY, NEED MORE

Do what big-time businesspeople do. Invest in something customers want. Sell your product for more than you paid. Here are some kid-sized investments that'll turn pennies into greenbacks.

566 **Invest in shoe-shine supplies.** Go door-to-door to shine shoes.

567 **Buy a bunch of flowers on Valentine's Day.** Put a red ribbon around each stem and sell the flowers one by one.

568 **Buy a bag of chocolate kisses on Valentine's Day.** Sell them one by one to kids in the neighborhood. Tell them to deliver the chocolate kisses with a real kiss!

569 **Buy blank tapes on sale.** Read aloud favorite children's books into a tape recorder then sell the tapes to parents of toddlers and young children.

570 **Make party tapes of favorite tunes and sell them to friends.**

571 **Buy large-size bags of snacks.** Repackage them into small lunch bags and sell them at the next local ball game.

572 **Buy a gallon of lemonade.** Sell it in small cups when people get thirsty after eating the small bags of snacks you sold them!

TO GRANDMOTHER'S HOUSE WE GO

Whether you're visiting your relatives or your relatives are visiting you, these ideas will help you make the most of it!

573 **Take along your Boredom Buster Bag.** Turn to #967–#976 for ideas of what to keep in it for emergencies. Visiting relatives with no kids or toys can be a real emergency!

574 **Take along mementos.** Relatives without children often enjoy looking at kids' collections, school photos, or school papers. Take them along to share when your grandparents or aunts and uncles ask: "How's school?" or "What's new?"

575 **Ask about the past.** Things were very different when your grandparents were young. Ask them to tell a story about the worst thing your parent did when he or she was your age. Ask what school was like, what games were played, what the old neighborhood was like.

576 **Learn something.** Ask your relative to teach you something from his or her childhood: a game, a song, a recipe, a skill.

577 **Go through old family albums.** Pretty soon you'll hear all the family scandals!

578 **Encourage your relatives to be show-offs.** Ask

them to show you their collections, toolbox, knick-knack cabinet, or jewelry box.

579 **Help out.** It's easier to talk to adults if you do something together than if you stare at each other from across the room.

580 **Make a family time line to pass the time.** On a long piece of paper fill out a time line with names, family events, and stories. This is a project most older relatives will love to help you with.

581 **Make a family tree.** Draw a big tree. Ask your relatives how to fill in the branches.

582 **Get out an almanac.** Sit down with your relatives and look on the map to see where faraway family members live.

❤ GO PLAY WITH YOUR COUSINS!

If you always get stuck playing with a bunch of younger cousins, try these ideas.

583 **Organize a game of "Sardine."** Choose one cousin to find a good hiding place. When he or she has hidden, the rest of the cousins search for the missing "sardine." As each cousin finds the sardine, he or she hides there, too, until all the cousins are squished into the hiding place like sardines in a can. The last cousin to join the group becomes the first sardine to hide in the next round.

584 **Send your cousins on a scavenger hunt.** Walk by yourself through the house or neighborhood. List objects for your cousins to find.

585 **Organize a game of "Pile-Up."** Challenge your cousins to see how many of them can pile up on top of each other. Don't try this on Aunt Tillie's antique rocking chair!

586 **Send your cousins into the bullring.** Choose one cousin, the bull, to go in the middle of a circle of cousins holding hands. The bull has to try to break out of the bullring and run away. If the bull gets loose, he or she tags another cousin to be the bull for the next round.

587 **If they're climbing all over you, take your cousins for a walk.** Tell them to collect seeds, pebbles, soda pop-tops — anything to unglue them from your leg!

588 **Get your cousins to button up.** Put all your cousins but one in a circle. Give one child in the circle a button. Those in the circle pass around the button as fast as possible so it's hard to see who has it. When you yell "Stop!" the cousin in the middle has to guess who's got the button. After a correct guess, whoever's holding the button goes in the middle and the game starts over.

589 **Family talk.** Put your cousins in a row. Whisper

something silly one of the grown-up relatives might have done. "Uncle Willie ate a pickle in Toonerville when a blue moose ran by." Each cousin whispers this to the next in line. The last cousin says the sentence out loud, which will probably sound a lot sillier than the original!

590 Try this knot game for little fingers. Organize your cousins into two equal teams. Give them each a length of string or rope with as many knots in it as team members. One by one, each team member has to untie one knot before passing the rope on to the next team member.

591 Quick change. Line up your cousins. Ask them to study you carefully. Then tell them to turn away from you. While they're not looking change one small thing about yourself — untie one shoe, roll down a sock, take off an earring, etc. — then ask everyone what you changed. The person who guesses gets to be the "quick change artist" for the next round.

592 It's some body! This requires extra-long rolls of paper. Cut the paper the length of each cousin. Hand them some markers and tell them to draw themselves on the paper.

593 Make a tent out of blankets and a table. Give your cousins some toys and animals and send them all inside the tent.

On a long bus ride, in the cafeteria, at your family meals — those are great times to start talking. Here are some ideas to get the conversation going.

594 **Predict the future.** Ask each person what they're going to be doing at different times in the future — one year, five years, etc.

595 **Good and bad.** Each person says one good and one bad thing that happened that day.

596 **Play "Now It Can Be Told."** Ask each person to reveal his or her most embarrassing moment.

597 **And now the news.** Have each person tell some news of the day. No bad news allowed!

598 **Ask parents about the good old days.** Find out what suppertime was like when your parents were children.

599 **Be nice.** Take turns saying one nice thing about each person.

600 **Find out everyone's favorite everything.** Get to know your friends' and family's favorites. Give each person a turn to tell his or her favorite color, favorite flavor, favorite book, movie, song, animal, sport, and hobby.

601 **Ask about work.** Ask your parents what's good

about their jobs and what's not. Talk about why you would or wouldn't like to do the same kind of job when you grow up.

602 **Be nosy.** Find out how your parents met, where they went on their first date, and what they liked best about each other when they first met.

603 **Ask about other names your parents almost called you.**

604 **Ask this question:** "If you were stuck on a faraway island and could only have one person, one book, and one other thing with you, who and what would they be?"

605 **Set up a tape recorder on New Year's Eve.** Ask everyone what his or her New Year's resolutions are for the next year. Play the tape back on December 31 next year.

606 **Make three wishes.** Ask everyone to make three wishes and share them. Maybe you can all figure out how to make some of them come true.

607 **Talk about what one thing you wish you could change.**

608 **Ask an adult to tell a true childhood story.**

 # ON THE SIDELINES

Before the game starts, or when you're stuck on the bench, here are some great ways to stay involved!

609 **Get ready to get into the game.** Stretch your muscles. Adjust knee pads. When you're on the bench, be ready to run in at a moment's notice.

610 **Make up a new cheer for each person on the team.** Something as simple as "Chris can't miss!" or "The ball went thataway. Whataway? Thataway!"

611 **Organize the sports equipment for your team.**

612 **Pay attention to the referee's calls.** This will help you avoid the same mistakes.

613 **Take notes.** Keep a notebook with points scored by each player. Figure out their batting averages, or yards gained and lost, or baskets made and missed.

614 **Watch the *other* team closely.** See if you can identify the weak spots in the team. Let your own team know whom to look out for.

615 **Take photos of the game, with the coach's permission.**

616 **Don't take being on the bench personally.** Think of at least two good reasons why you have to sit out — too many players is one big reason.

617 **Think of five reasons you're glad to be on the bench.**

618 **Think of your favorite sports heroes.** They started out on the bench, too, before their coaches discovered how great they really were.

619 **Think about a teammate who sat out last time.** Cheer extra hard for him or her.

620 **Make up a team roster.** Write down every player's name, shirt number, and position played. Make copies for the next game and hand them out to fans.

621 **Get the ball when it goes out-of-bounds.** Return it swiftly and accurately.

622 **Draw a "dream uniform" for your team.**

623 **Think of a new name for your team.**

624 **Draw a team mascot.**

WAITING ON TABLES

What do you do when you're in a restaurant and the food takes forever to come?

625 **Take bets on when your food's going to arrive.**

626 **Play squiggles on place mats.** Draw some stray lines and ask the person next to you to turn them into a picture.

627 **Have a live caterpillar as your main course.** Scrunch the paper wrapper down around your straw as far as it will go. Pull it off and wet it drop by drop with water from your straw. Just a few drops and your paper "caterpillar" will come to life.

628 **Bring a spider to dinner.** Peel down strips from each end of your straw wrapper, leaving the wrapper whole at the center. Twist each of the strips into "legs." Drip a couple of drops of water on each "leg" of your paper spider. Watch it crawl across the table!

629 See who can come closest to guessing how much the check will be.

630 See who can figure out the tip the fastest.

✏ LONG LINES — THE WAIT YOU LOVE TO HATE

Movie lines, museum lines, amusement-park lines, any lines. They're all boring to be stuck in, unless you have this list with you!

631 Pass the time people-watching. First, count how many people are in front of you.

632 Count how many people are behind you.

633 Count how many people are wearing something red.

634 How many people are wearing sneakers?

635 Find the tallest person in the line.

636 Find the smallest person in the line.

637 How many people have blond hair?

638 How many people have brown hair?

639 How many people have red hair?

640 How many people have black hair?

641 How many people have little or no hair?

642 Who is the loudest person in the line?

643 Count how many people stand on tiptoes to see over the person ahead.

644 Count the freckles on the back of the neck in front of you.

645 Draw finger pictures on the backs of friends waiting in line with you. Have your friend guess what you drew, then switch.

646 Make up a "life story" for each person in the line. Think about where they might have been born, what their parents might be like, what they will do when they grow up or what they do if they are grown-up already.

647 Yawn. See how many people in the line you can make yawn, too.

648 Count how many people get in the door or gate every five seconds.

649 Smile at someone in the line. See how many people you can make smile back at you.

650 Wriggle. Wriggle your toes. Wriggle your fingers. Stand on tiptoe. Stand flat, then back and forth ten times. Roll your head around to relax your neck. Pretend you're in the Olympics warming up before your event.

651 Close your eyes for sixty seconds. Open them and see if the line moved ahead without you.

652 Compare lines. In your mind, compare this line to the longest line you've ever waited in. If it's shorter, feel grateful. If not, think about *this* line on the next line you wait in.

When in line at tourist attractions or museums:

653 Count the different accents and foreign languages you hear in the line.

654 Read a book or brochure about the place you're visiting.

655 In your mind, create the perfect souvenir for this place.

♥ **BUSY ON THE BUS**

Riding the bus back and forth to school is about as exciting as dust settling on a counter. Add a little zip to the trip with these quick tips.

656 **Write backward messages.** Breathe on the window and try to write a backward message in the steam. Write Ǝ⅃IMƧ , then watch people in cars to see who does.

657 **Have a staring contest** with the person in the seat next to you.

658 **Play "Bus Line."** Whisper a message to the person next to you and say "Pass it on." The last person to receive the message says it aloud. Chances are it won't be the same as the message you first said.

659 Count the number of bumps your bus goes over

from school to your bus stop. The next day, close your eyes when the bus leaves the school. Start counting bumps to see if you can open your eyes exactly at your stop just by counting bumps.

660 **Make a sign for vehicles behind the bus.** It might say: "Laugh if you love the smell of bus exhaust!"

661 **Make an anagram out of your name.** Write your name and rearrange the letters in it to spell another word or phrase. For example: "Anne Smith" could be "means thin."

662 **Play "Two for Two" with the person next to you.** In the time it takes to get to school, each person writes down as many twosomes as he or she knows. Start with Hansel and Gretel, Batman and Robin, or Jack and Jill. The player with the most pairs wins.

663 **Name that tune!** In how many notes can you name a tune? Have the person next to you hum as few notes as possible until you guess the song. Take turns humming and guessing. The person with the fewest notes wins.

664 **Play "Rumpelstiltskin."** In three tries, see if you can guess the middle name of the bus driver. Each rider gets three guesses.

665 **Start a paper pass.** Don't throw a paper ball, just pass it hand to hand. See how many times the ball can get passed around the bus and back to you before you arrive at school.

666 **Write a "Thank you for the ride" note to the bus driver.** He or she will really appreciate it!

667 **Have a silent contest.** Don't talk for the whole trip. No laughing, either!

668 **Talk to your hand.** Make a fist, draw eyes and a top lip on your index finger, and a bottom lip on your thumb. Move your folded-in thumb up and down to make your *hand*-some friend "talk."

669 **Have a conversation with the person next to you.** Count how many times he or she says, "you know?" or "like," or "and ah." Tell your friend the final count. Then switch and see if it's possible for you to talk without using any of those phrases.

670 **Tease a friend.** Brain-tease a friend, that is. Ask how many different three-letter words can be made out of the word THE. Give up? None!

671 **Count the freckles on one arm.** If you have a lot of them, play connect-the-freckles with a washable ink pen. Study the finished shape and try to figure out what it is.

672 **Have a Funny Face Contest.** The funniest face gets to make that face at the window to other cars going by.

673 **Read palms.** Ask the person next to you if he or she would like his or her palm read. If the answer is yes, hold the outstretched palm, study it for a few seconds, then draw a long red line across it with a red pen. Voilà! The palm is red!

674 **Start a Rhyme-Go-Round.** You begin with "I

have a cat who is very fat." The next person must add to the rhyme. For example: "I have a cat who is very fat and wears a hat." Keep adding to the rhyme until the bus stops.

675 Start a story. Write the opening line to a story at the top of a sheet of paper. Give it to the person next to you who writes the second line and folds down your line so only the second line shows for the third person. Kids keep adding a line to the previous line that shows. When the story makes it back to you, read the whole story aloud to everyone on the bus.

676 Make up five more things for the busy-on-the-bus category.

 # CAR POOL CAPERS

Too bad you can't swim in the car pool! But you can play these games in it, and you won't need a bathing suit!

677 Take a guess. Guess how many red lights the driver will get. Guess how many school buses the car will get stuck behind. Guess how many minutes the trip will take.

678 Be a spooky DJ and play ghost story tapes for the rest of the car. Stop the tape right before the end so everyone else can guess the ending. If there's no tape deck in the car, be a spooky storyteller and read from your favorite horror stories.

679 **Pick one car pool day as Make-a-Face Day, when nobody talks but everybody makes faces!**

680 **Have Joke Day once a week.**

681 **Have Solve-a-Crime Day.** Get mini-mysteries from the library. (*Encyclopedia Brown* books are great for this.) Have someone read the mystery and see how fast the car pool can solve it before the end of the trip.

682 **Assign a Greatest Hits Day.** On a person's assigned day, he or she brings along a favorite tape to play for the car pool.

683 **Write notes in reverse to the driver.** Hold up your message so the driver can read it in the rearview mirror.

684 **Stuck in traffic? Try finger tapping.** Finger tap the rhythm of well-known songs like "On Top of Old Smokey" or "Mary Had a Little Lamb." The person who guesses the finger-tap song is the next tapper.

☆ **BACKSEAT BLUES**

Stuck in the backseat on a long, long car ride? Try one or two of these bored-in-the-backseat blues breakers.

685 **Have a backseat sing-along.** Bring a tape recorder or Walkman and a collection of your old song tapes from when you were younger. Play all the songs — "Old MacDonald," "The Wheels on the Bus," "B-I-N-G-O," "Eentzy-Weentzy Spider," and sing along. You know all the words, and so will everyone else.

686 **Play backseat bingo.** You can play by yourself or with another bored seatmate. Make up bingo cards with many of the same items, but some different ones, on each card. Mark the items off as you see them out the window. First one to get a row completed or fill the whole card wins. Include commonly seen items such as blue car, stop sign, police car, rest stop, personalized license plate, moving van, etc.

687 **Spot a sign.** Keep count of how many hospital signs you see between your home and your destination.

688 **Figure out fast-food stops.** Write down the number of miles on the odometer at the beginning of the trip. Count how many miles are between each McDonald's (or other fast-food chain) restaurant. See who can come closest to guessing the mile mark of the next restaurant.

689 **Honk, honk!** See how many truck drivers will honk their horns for you. The sign for honking is one hand moving up and down in the air, as if pulling on a rope.

690 **Watch the speed.** Keep an eye on the speedometer. See how close to the speed limit the driver can stay.

691 **Give the driver a neck rub.**

692 **Look for one-of-a-kind sightings.** List anything strange or unusual in a travel journal.

693 **Count how many old tires or tire parts you see along the highway.**

694 **Play an "I-Spy" game.** Think up some categories then look for them: chickens in a yard, lawn statues, billboards, a farmer on a tractor, scarecrows, etc.

695 **Read a book that takes place where you're going.**

696 **Follow the map of your trip.** Check off small towns as you pass them.

697 **Smile at people in other cars.** Make sure you have an orange section stuck over your teeth when you do!

698 **Wave to other kids stuck in the backseat.**

699 **Make signs to other kids stuck in the backseat.** Write a question you want answered by someone in another car.

700 **Play "Alphaplates."** Beginning with the letter "A," call out letters of the alphabet as you spot them on a license plate. You can only call out letters in alphabetical order.

701 **Play "They're So Vain."** See who can spot the most vanity license plates (you know, the plates with the nicknames, cute and not-always-so-cute sayings) before you get to where you're going.

702 **Make your own top-ten hits on a long trip.** Tape songs by putting the tape recorder next to backseat speakers.

703 **Ask your parents to tell you about their childhood car trips.**

CITY SIDEWALKS, BUSY SIDEWALKS

Take a hike! Instead of hitching a ride, take to the streets.

704 **Side walk on the sidewalk.** That's right. Walk sideways instead of straight ahead. You'll get a new view and show everyone a new side of yourself.

705 **Be a meter person.** Look for coins people drop on the ground next to parking meters.

706 **Be a meter reader.** If you find some coins, do overdue parkers a favor and drop in a coin so they won't get a ticket.

707 **Collect coins.** Check the return slot in all the pay phones you pass. Add up your coins and call a friend.

708 **Get a free soda.** See if you can find coins in the slots of soda machines. If you find enough of them, treat yourself to a soda.

709 **Power walk.** Take a stopwatch and see if you can get the same old errands done in less time.

710 **Brighten up city streets.** Plant a flower seed somewhere along a regular walking route. Water it, watch it, weed it, then enjoy your "offspring" whenever you go by.

711 **Play "What's a Pennyworth?"** Drop a penny on a busy sidewalk. Count how many people go by before someone picks up the penny.

712 **Hide a coin in a busy place you pass often.** Every time you pass the spot, check to see if your coin is still there.

713 **Take an Alphabet Walk with a friend.** Call out the names of objects you spot, in alphabetical order.

714 **Get in shape.** When you run out of the alphabet, look for objects in a particular shape.

715 **Play "Hat Trick."** Stand on a busy corner and count how many people are wearing hats. Then count how many people have them on backward.

716 **Look for window watchers.** When you pass tall office buildings, check out how many people are staring out the window instead of working.

717 **Look for people talking.** After you count window watchers, count how many people are talking on phones in their offices.

718 **Offer a penny for thoughts.** Tell people at a bus stop or in a store line that you're paying a penny for thoughts. Ask what they're thinking right at that moment. Thank those who answer and give them a penny.

719 **See if yellow means caution.** Count how many cars go through yellow lights instead of stopping or slowing down.

720 **Count jaywalkers, but don't be one.** See how many people cross the street against the light.

721 **Stay on the beat.** Keep an eye on how long it takes for a police officer to ticket double-parked cars.

✏ WHAT'S IN STORE?

Store up some fun even when you don't have a cent in your pocket. You don't need a dime to browse, window-shop, or compare prices. All you need is time and a few ideas of how to shop when there's no money to shop with.

722 **Window-shop.** No, you're not going to buy some windows, just judge how they look. Award points to shop windows on a scale of 1 (Don't bother looking!) to 10 (Wow! I'm going inside!). See how many people go by the dull windows without looking and how many stop to look at the tempting ones.

723 **Guess the most expensive item in a store.** Walk through a store with a friend and check out the merchandise. See if you can guess which item costs the most. Then compare price tags and see who found the all-time budget buster.

724 **Guess the most popular item in a store.** Then find the manager and ask what item customers buy most often.

725 **Plan birthday and holiday shopping early.** On a slow day at your favorite store, walk through and write down items you might want to give as presents in the future.

726 **Budget-shop.** Give yourself a small budget — or a huge one — and see how many things you can "buy" in your favorite store within your budget. Then go home and read #521–#529 and #548–#572 on ways to earn money to buy what's on your list.

❤ WHILE STROLLING THROUGH THE PARK ONE DAY

If all the noise and the crowds are getting to you, head for the green. Take a walk to your local park. Park yourself there for a while, and pass the time.

727 **Be a wheel watcher.** Sit on a bench and count how many people go by on Rollerblades, bikes, or in strollers.

728 **Check for safety.** What percentage of Rollerbladers and bikers wear helmets or knee and elbow pads?

729 **Be a hot dogger.** Find a bench next to a hot-dog cart. How many hot dogs does the hot-dog vendor sell in fifteen minutes?

730 **Do a wildlife count.** Are there more dogs walking in the park or more squirrels? More pigeons or people?

731 **Test the equipment.** Try out every piece of equipment on the playground. Enjoy.

732 **Feed the ducks.** No ducks? Feed the pigeons. Or find the park snack bar or wagon and feed yourself!

733 **Find water.** There you will find people drinking from fountains, sitting near fountains, feeding ducks, playing with sailboats. Sit on a nearby bench and watch the people.

734 **Go to the dogs.** Dog-watch the dog-walkers when you're tired of people-watching. Do dog-walkers look like their dogs? Are short people with little dogs, or just the opposite? Do neat-looking people have well-trimmed dogs and shaggy people have shaggy dogs?

SEE 'EM IN THE MUSEUM

Art museums, natural history museums, space museums, all museums have one thing in common: lots to see! Here are some tips to make your visit extra interesting and extra fun!

735 Look for the oldest exhibit item in the whole museum.

736 Ask one of the guards to tell you about the funniest thing he or she ever saw a museum visitor do.

737 **Collect free brochures.** Most museums hand out printed information about their exhibits. Take them and keep them in a souvenir box at home.

738 Keep a notebook with you and write down your top-ten favorite things in the museum.

739 **Watch the other museum visitors.** People are just as interesting as the exhibits!

740 **Be a museum statue.** Find a spot in an exhibit room where you can stand perfectly still, posed as a statue of the world's most famous kid. See how many people notice you.

741 **Join a group tour in progress.** Stay next to them long enough to learn three new things about the exhibits.

742 **Redesign an exhibit.** Choose an exhibit that you think could be displayed better. Think how you might change the lighting, the background colors, the arrangement of the articles in the display.

743 **Count how many kids look bored at the museum.**

744 **After you've seen all you can see in the museum, find the gift shop!** You be the judge about which exhibit has the best souvenirs.

745 **Sit down for two minutes and rest.** Wriggle your toes in your shoes. Wriggle your fingers. Close your eyes. Yawn. Open your eyes. Stand up and continue your museum tour.

746 **Choose one painting, statue, object, or display as your absolute favorite in the museum.** Read all the labels that are on or by it. Find out everything you can about it. Tell a friend or family member why you recommend seeing this one thing above all else.

747 **Ask a guard or information-desk person for a recommendation of the best things to see if a person only has fifteen minutes to visit.** Then find those things.

748 **Do a museum review.** On the way home from the museum, have each person in your group tell one favorite thing seen in the museum. How about their *least* favorite? Why?

☆ ROOM WITH A VIEW

If you live in the city, you can find some fun in the sights before and below your eyes. A view from a window can be the "eye-deal" way to pass the time away.

749 Find out how far "far as the eye can see" really is. What is the farthest thing you can see clearly from where you're looking out?

750 Look through a pair of binoculars. Now what is the farthest thing you notice?

751 Count how many people look up at you or your building as they walk by.

752 Catch the litterbugs. Watch to see how many people drop litter on the sidewalk or street.

753 Count how many people are carrying a long loaf of French or Italian bread.

754 Be a Neighborhood Watch Kid. Watch the building across the street to see who goes in and who comes out.

755 Take notes on what you see. Write down the funniest sights, the most surprising sights, and the most unusual sights. Put them all down in a notebook.

756 Be a Fashion Finder. Keep a record of the colors most often worn by people passing by. Try to spot new fads such as new haircuts, shoe styles, and clothes styles.

757 Count taxicabs.

758 Count people walking their dogs.

759 Look at the sky and find all the clouds that are shaped like animals.

760 Draw a picture of the building across the street.

761 Make a "Hi!" sign. Put a sign in *your* window for someone else who is looking out *their* window to see.

762 Write a poem about the view from your window.

✍ TIRED OF YOUR ROOM?

How about these room-gloom remedies?

763 Switch rooms with your brother or sister. Not forever. Just long enough for you to start missing your old room.

764 Make your bed upside down. Put the pillow at the other end and sleep with your head at the foot of the bed instead.

765 Remove one piece of furniture from your room. Don't fill the new empty space. Enjoy it.

766 Move all the furniture against the walls. The room will look bigger.

767 Move your bed to the middle of a too-big room. It will look cozier.

768 Don't decorate your room, decorate your ceiling! Tape some of your favorite posters onto the ceiling above your bed. See. Things are looking up already!

769 **Move your furniture around every day for a week.** Spend a night with it each new way. Stick with the arrangement you like best.

770 **Put a black-construction-paper cat silhouette in your window.** Doesn't that look cozy?

771 **Tape colored plastic wrap over each pane of window glass.** When the sun shines through, your window will have a stained glass look.

772 **Hang sun catchers or prisms in your window.** The sun will dance around your room, giving you a real light show to watch.

773 **Paint a design on your window shade.** Use acrylic paints to add a giant smiling face or sun, a midnight sky with a moon crescent and white stars around it, polka dots, butterflies, a rainbow, or whatever you like.

774 **Make some Memory Pillows to toss around your room.** Save T-shirts that mean a lot to you — from camp, from a sports uniform, from school, from a vacation place. Tuck in and stitch up the sleeves and neck opening. Stuff with cotton batting and stitch up the bottom. Your pillows will bring back good memories, and they'll fit your room to a T!

775 **Add life to your room.** Start a plant collection. Some people even talk to their plants! Go ahead — talk to them! Say, "How's leaf treating you?"

776 Make a wall mural. Using a roll of brown package-wrapping paper or white paper, roll out a section to go across one wall. Paint, or use markers, to make a scene. Have your friends autograph it and write silly things when they visit. Make it a work-in-progress, allowing anyone who comes in to add whatever they want.

777 Make a dish garden of a few pretty cacti. They don't talk back and hardly need any water.

778 Turn your room into a gallery. Hang string across the top of one wall. Clip your latest artwork with clothespins attached to the string.

779 Create a photo wall. Hang pictures of your family, friends, pets, teachers, and yourself all on one wall.

780 Hide your stuff in an old dresser drawer under the bed. Your room will thank you.

781 Don't change your room, change what you do in your room. Turn on music and dance. Turn off music and just sit and meditate. Make it a club-meeting room. Make it a reading room. Make it an exercise room.

782 Give your door a do-over. Cover it with posters or funny signs.

NEED A NEW LOOK?

Design something to wear that no one else has!

783 **Wear your jewelry or buttons on your baseball hat.** Nobody else will have a hat quite like that.

784 **Adopt one neon color.** Look for hats, shoelaces, pins, and accessories in that color so people know when you come into a room.

785 **Glue fake jewels onto your sneakers.**

786 **Paint plain sneakers with neon fabric paint.** Color coordinate with some shoelaces.

787 **Decorate your most boring hairbands.**

788 **Spice up your boring T-shirts with fabric paint.**

789 **Paint stencils on your plain sweatshirts.** You'll find easy-to-paint stencils in paint and crafts stores. They're usually for walls and furniture, but with fabric paint you can use them to jazz up a sweatshirt.

790 **Find a tiny wash-off tattoo that's you.** Wear it on the inside of your wrist.

791 **Go ahead.** Get a haircut that's different from all your friends'. If you change your mind, don't worry — it'll grow back.

HACKING AROUND ON YOUR COMPUTER

You've gotten into the wizard's castle. You've even knocked off a couple of book reports on your PC. But there's so much more to do with your computer.. . .

792 Start a monthly one-page neighborhood classified ad sheet.

793 Design personalized stationery for family, friends, and neighbors.

794 Start a family newspaper. Ask faraway relatives to send news for the paper.

795 Create name banners for friends' bedroom doors.

796 Type up mailing labels from people's address books. They'll be so useful at holiday, birthday, and vacation times.

797 Create grocery checklists for your parents.

798 Design holiday and birthday coupon books.

799 Design several styles of party invitations. Show them around. Take orders.

800 Start an outrageous tabloid newspaper. (SPACE ALIEN RUNS FOR PRESIDENT!) Sell it to kids your age.

PICTURE THIS

Don't be camera shy. Be a hot shot. Get out some rolls of film and roll 'em. Here are some great ideas to try with your camera.

801 **Picture yourself.** Take self-portraits in new ways — reflected in store windows, chrome bumpers, puddles, any reflective surface.

802 **Ham it up.** Take pictures of your friends making their craziest faces.

803 **Color your world.** Take pictures of objects that are your favorite color around your house, the neighborhood, or town.

804 **Make your own school yearbook.** Throughout the school year, take candid shots of your friends and teachers around school. Get extra copies and put them into small albums that you can make out of sheets of construction paper stapled together. At the end of the year you can sell them to classmates or give them to friends as gifts.

805 **Take shadow pictures.** On a late, sunny day, take pictures of nothing but shadows. Ask your friends to stretch, run, hop, leap, and stand on their heads, then photograph their shadows.

806 **Take extreme close-ups of objects around your neighborhood.** Shoot close-ups of doorknockers, knotholes on trees, cracks in the sidewalks —

things you see every day but never really noticed. Then show the pictures to friends and see if they can guess what the objects are.

807 **Be a party photographer.** Hire yourself out to take pictures at kids' birthday parties. Take lots of pictures that include the parents, too.

808 **Take close-ups of your favorite things.** Arrange some of your favorite possessions on a tabletop and make a still-life photo.

809 **Take three shots of the same subject.** Shoot a subject close-up, from a middle distance, then from far away.

810 **Repeat that.** Shoot a roll of pictures of nothing but patterns filling the frame: grids over the sidewalk, a stack of pipes or lumber, cars parked in a lot, a bed of tulips, a fruit display, a row of soup cans at the store.

811 **Get a head.** On a large sheet of poster board, paint a giant picture of an animal with no head — a monkey, a cat, a rooster. Cut out a head-sized oval. Then pose your friends behind the cutout.

812 **Heads up.** This time do it the other way. Take head shots of friends, cut them out, paste them on small poster board, then draw a silly *body* underneath.

813 **Lights, camera, action.** If you stand sideways to moving objects, you'll get a blurred sense of action. Catch people on the move in cars, on bikes, throwing balls, marching, etc.

814 **Figure out the angle.** Shoot familiar objects (or people) from odd angles and see if your friends can guess your subjects.

815 **Find the hidden face.** Does the parking meter downtown look like your Uncle Joe? Does the doorway and two windows above it in the house across the street look like someone yawning? Photograph objects that look like faces.

816 **Play "Fun House."** Hold or place a piece of rippled glass between your camera and a friend's face, then click. You'll swear the pictures were taken in the house of mirrors.

817 **Watch a photo finish.** Go to a one-hour photo developing place with a roll of film. Stick around and watch your pictures get developed.

☆ WHEN THERE'S NOTHING TO DO, LEARN SOMETHING NEW

Try something you've always wanted to do but never knew how. Often all it takes is a little practice (and sometimes a friendly person to help you out).

818 **Learn how to eat with chopsticks.** Practice until you don't drop even one grain of rice.

819 Learn how to throw a curveball.

820 Learn to roller skate.

821 Learn to ice skate.

822 Learn how to crack an egg without getting any shell in it.

823 Learn how to make one breakfast and one lunch you like.

824 Learn how to tape a show on your VCR.

825 Learn how to wash windows without leaving streaks on the glass.

826 Learn how to plant flowers in a flowerpot.

827 Learn how to make a salad.

828 Learn how to use the electric blender to make cool summer shakes.

829 Learn a new word in the dictionary and use it at dinnertime.

830 Learn a foreign word.

831 Learn how to hammer a nail in straight.

832 Learn how to take a good photograph.

833 Learn how to play a new board game.

834 Learn how to wiggle your ears.

835 Learn how to stand on your head.

836 Learn how to swim.

837 Learn how to breathe properly when you're running so you won't get a cramp.

838 Learn how to play tennis.

839 Learn how to eat a taco without having everything in it fall out.

840 Learn how to look a person right in the eye

and give a good, firm handshake as you say, "Nice to meet you."

841   Learn how to fold a fitted sheet.

842   Learn how to do hospital corners when you make your bed.

843   Learn how to pack a suitcase.

844   Learn how to sew on a button.

845   Learn how to fix a hem that's coming down.

846   Learn how to bait your own fishhook.

847   Learn how to stand up straight.

848   Learn how to blow the biggest bubble with bubble gum.

849   Learn how to keep a calendar of all your activities and deadlines.

850   Learn how to change the water in the fish tank.

851   Learn how to play one song on a piano even if you're not taking lessons.

852   Learn how to twirl spaghetti using a fork and a soupspoon.

 # ONE THING LEADS TO ANOTHER

There are some jobs everybody hates, but you've got to do them. Get a bad job over with then treat yourself royally.

853 **Sort out your shoes and sneakers.** Then put on your favorite old slippers.

854 **Organize your bookshelves.** Then reread your favorite picture book.

855 **Clean out your school notebook.** Then call up a favorite school friend.

856 **Clean up the dishes.** Save your dessert till after the job is done.

857 **Hang up or put away all the clothes that are lying around.** Then pick out your favorite outfit to wear the next day.

858 **Clean out the pile from under your bed.** Then dust off and use one of the forgotten things you found under there.

859 **Complete your address book with current addresses and phone numbers of friends and family.** Then write to a favorite person in your book.

860 **Spend a half hour working on a skill you're trying to master.** Then show off what you practiced.

861 **Clean out your school book bag.** Then pick it up. There, isn't it easier to carry now?

BE A COLLECTO-MANIAC!

Collecting can be lots of fun — and here are some great ideas on how to get started.

862 **Collect something. Anything.** Decide what it is you want to collect. Choose your favorite animal, let's say it's a squirrel. Tell everyone you know that you collect squirrels — stuffed, stickers, earrings, posters, etc. Be sure to choose something you really like, because when the word gets out that you're starting a collection, people will want to add to it.

863 **Make a list of possible collection ideas.** Try listing things from A to Z. Or just list things that are free, such as gum wrappers, ticket stubs, birthday cards, rocks, beach glass, shells, recipes, or bottle caps. Get a friend to collect what you collect, and you'll have hours of fun sharing, comparing, and adding to each others' collections, too.

864 **Set up a collection center.** A good collection deserves good storage space — a shelf, a clear plastic box, a binder, a bulletin board, or a drawer. You can display your collections on mobiles, chains, sculptures, or collages. Keep a notebook nearby to record where you get things, how much you paid, or who gave a collection item to you. Then when you're ready to trade, you can make sure you give and get a fair deal.

865 **Collect beads or buttons.** Fancy, colored, plain, plastic, metal, or cloth-covered. They're fun to find, fun to save, and easy to keep in a tin box or glass jar. Just enjoy looking at them or use them in various craft activities.

866 **Collect baseball cards.** Study *Beckett* magazine for the current values and prices of all the cards. Make trades or purchases carefully. Baseball cards can be worth a lot of money.

867 **Collect stickers.** They're everywhere, even in cereal boxes. Keep your collection in an album or loose in boxes. Organize them by subject, value, type. Remember to pick up souvenir stickers on vacation.

868 **Plan a Sticker Swap-Meet Party.** This is a good way to build your collection.

869 **Collect aluminum can pop-tops.** Make a chain long enough to go all the way around your room twice. You can't trade these, but they're always easy to find.

870 **Collect message buttons.** You know, the ones that make people think when they read them. Pin them onto a bulletin board, or hang up a denim jacket or T-shirt and display them there. Find buttons with pictures of your favorite rock groups, political campaign buttons, advertising buttons, all buttons. You can build a big collection fast. These kinds of buttons are everywhere.

871 **Collect toys.** Trolls. Matchbox cars. Dolls. Whatever makes your collection shelf look good. Garage and tag sales are great sources for old toys. Older brothers and sisters of your friends might feel like giving some of their old toys away. Take them!

872 **Collect coins.** Check their value in a coin-collecting guide. Or just collect any coins made the year you were born.

873 **Collect business cards wherever you go.** Many of them have pretty designs, funny sayings, and offer one-of-a-kind products and services. Keep them in a photo album.

874 **Collect charms.** You know, those little plastic or metal miniatures that look just like the real thing, only tiny. Wear your charms on a necklace or bracelet, or keep them in a box with small compartments. A charming idea, really!

875 **Collect key chains.** Everywhere you go you'll find key chains with different designs and messages on them. Companies give them away as advertising premiums. Tourist places sell them. They're everywhere.

876 **Collect china or glass figures.** Horses, cats, dogs, frogs, rabbits, and just about everything else come in cute little poses ready to turn your collecting cabinet into a menagerie. This is a collection to keep forever.

877 **Collect erasers.** They come in all different shapes, from ice-cream cones to soccer balls to unicorns. Erasers are fun to collect and use. You can display them on a bulletin board with straight pins.

878 **Collect picture postcards.** Don't worry if you never go any farther than the corner store. Even your own town probably sells postcards, and so does every other place where people go to visit. Tell everyone you know to drop you a postcard from wherever they go. Your collection will help you see the world without even leaving your house!

879 **Collect pencil toppers.** Favorite comic strip characters, movie characters, cartoon stars, holiday themes, sports equipment — every object you can think of has shown up on pencils where erasers used to be. Put each one on a pencil. Display the pencils in a big jar or glass.

880 **Collect books.** Choose some favorite authors and collect every book ever written by them. Add books about the authors to your collection, too. A book collection is the beginning of a library you'll want to keep forever. Maybe someday you'll even pass it on to your own children!

881 **Collect bird nests.** Make sure the birds have flown away, of course! Bird nests are beautiful, each one different. Put some big branches into a tall vase. Display your nests on the branches.

882 **Collect leaves.** Look for leaves from all different plants. Use a plant book to help you identify the leaves. Press them between two pieces of waxed paper. Keep them flat and perfect in an album, or make beautiful leaf collages to give as gifts. Place mats made with leaves pressed between two pieces of clear Con-Tac paper show your leaves off perfectly.

883 **Collect pressed flowers.** You can collect, press, and save them the same way you do leaves.

884 **Collect jokes.** Every time you hear a new joke, write it down on an index card. Organize your "joke file" by subject matter — animal jokes, doctor jokes, waiter jokes. Keep the cards in file boxes. Famous comedians have joke files, too. Who knows? Maybe your collection will put you in the spotlight someday!

885 **Collect autographs.** This is easier to do than you might think. You can write to any television, recording, or movie star in care of the station, recording company, or movie company. Very often you will even get an autographed picture if you request one.

886 **Collect beautiful hairbands.** When they aren't on your head, display them on a towel rack in your room.

887 **Collect jewelry pins.** Display them on your favorite teddy bears.

888 **Collect barrettes.** Decorate the hair of your favorite long-haired doll as a clever way to display them.

889 **Collect rings.** Display each one in its own clear plastic compartment.

890 **Collect trophies, ribbons, and award certificates.** Dedicate a shelf and wall space around it. Look at your collection whenever you're feeling down on yourself.

891 **Collect school pictures of all your friends.** Tape them all to one big poster board and hang it up on your wall.

♥ # AN EMPTY JAR CAN BE FULL OF FUN

When your day seems as empty as the glass jars in the recycling bin, save the jars and save the day with some of these activities.

892 **Make an Ocean-in-a-Jar.** Use a big glass jar — pickle jars, mayonnaise, or jelly jars are good. Fill the jar about three quarters full of water. Add a few drops of blue food coloring. Add baby oil until the jar is almost filled. Put the lid on very tightly. Shake it up and turn the jar from side to side. You'll see the ocean wave. Go ahead — wave back!

893 Put pretty shells in a jar.

894 **Make a sand sculpture.** At a crafts store buy several different colors of sand. Use a clean, clear jar. Pour in layers of different-colored sand. You can make designs on the sides by poking a tooth-pick or nail down the sides, allowing the color above to drain into the hole. Fill the jar, put the top on, and keep it on your desk as a pretty decoration.

895 **Group your Ocean-in-a-Jar, shell jar, and sand sculpture jars together.** Now you have a beach!

896 **Have a Beans-in-a-Jar Guessing Game.** Ask someone else to fill a jar with jelly beans. The person should count exactly how many beans are in the jar. You and your friends take turns guessing the number. The winner gets the jar full of jelly beans!

897 **Make decorated storage containers for the kitchen.** Get four jars in graduated sizes from small to medium to large to extra-large. After you clean them out, use acrylic paints to paint designs on the jars or put labels on saying what they could hold — sugar, flour, tea bags, powdered ice-tea mix, nuts, or candy. These make great gifts!

898 **Make a bank.** Have someone who's handy with tools make a coin slot in the lid. Keep the jar where people are sure to see it. People can't resist dropping a penny into a jar. Try it, and you'll see!

899 **Store your marbles in a jar.** Keep the jar on the windowsill so the sun can shine through and catch the beautiful colors.

900 **Play "Straw-in-the-Jar."** Stand directly over an open jar so that, when you look down, the jar is right at the tips of your toes. Pick up a straw and hold it near your nose, above the jar opening. Drop the straw. See how many out of five land in the jar.

901 **Store your minis in a maxi jar.** Fill a big jar with your tiniest, hard-to-find toys. Matchbox cars, mini dolls, figures, beads, or any small things you collect will fit right in a big jar.

902 **Play "Penny-Pitch" with a friend.** Take turns trying to pitch pennies into an open jar.

903 **Make a night-light out of a jar filled with lightning bugs.** Collect as many as you can and put them in the jar. Make sure there are air holes in the lid. Hold the jar under the covers. After a short while, take the jar outside and release the bugs.

904 **Save time in a jar.** Make a time capsule. Fill a jar with a recent photo of you and your best friend, one thing from your collections, a souvenir of a trip you took recently, funny notes passed to you in school, pictures of your favorite stars, a slip of paper telling your age, height, weight, and what you want to be when you grow up. Close the jar and put it away on your top closet shelf, in the attic, or somewhere you won't see it for a long time. Do not open for at least one year — five years would even be better.

905 **Fill small jars with water.** Add a few drops of food coloring to each jar, making each one a different color. Line the jars up on a windowsill to work as sun catchers.

906 **Shoot marbles into a jar on its side.**

907 **Make up funny labels for empty jars.** Fill them with colored water, cotton, or something else and put them in food cabinets for someone else to find. Here are some laughable label ideas: TRAF-FIC JAM, CHOCOLATE COVERED WORMS, CATER-PILLAR HELPER. Make up some more of your own.

 # SNACK ATTACK!

Uh-oh. There's nothing good to have for a snack, and you're hungry! What kind of snacks could you possibly make out of what's on hand? Try these!

908 **Make a chocolate dip.** Warm up bottled chocolate syrup. Dip in sponge or pound cake, banana slices, vanilla wafer cookies, doughnut pieces, or strawberries.

909 **Core an apple.** Fill the space with peanut butter. Cut the apple into sections. Yum-yum!

910 **Shake up things.** You don't need ice cream to make a great shake. In a blender, mix one cup of milk, one banana, one-half teaspoon sugar, and five ice cubes. Blend for one minute for a thick, creamy shake.

911 **Change recipes.** Take a favorite recipe and alter the ingredients a little to see if you can make the dish even better!

912 **Make cinnamon toast fingers.** Spread margarine or butter on bread. Mix together four tablespoons of sugar and one teaspoon of cinnamon. Sprinkle the mixture on the buttered bread. Toast top only on a tray in a toaster oven.

913 **Dip it.** Peel a carrot and dip it into grape jelly.

914 **Fill it.** Fill celery stalks with cream cheese, cheddar cheese spread, or peanut butter.

915 **Make easy pizza.** Spread pizza sauce or spaghetti sauce on each half of a muffin. Sprinkle with shredded mozzarella or cheddar cheese. Toast top only on a tray in the toaster oven.

916 **Make a snow cone.** Crush ice in a blender. Cover with any fruit-flavored syrup.

917 **Juice up.** Freeze an ice-cube tray full of your favorite juice. Eat the mini-juice cubes or use them to dress up a glass of juice.

918 **Be a honey.** Drip honey over a rolled-up chunk of cream cheese.

919 **Be sweet, but not too sweet.** Mix together Goldfish crackers, raisins, and mini-marshmallows.

920 **Top this.** Spread peanut butter on Graham crackers and cover with marshmallow topping.

921 **Make a minisalad.** Cut up one apple into cubes, add one tablespoon each of mayonnaise, raisins, and chopped walnuts. Voilà!

922 **Egg yourself on.** Hard-boil some eggs. Peel one, dip into salt, and eat up!

923 **Make dare-devil eggs.** Cut a hard-boiled egg in half, take out the yoke and mash it with mayonnaise and a dab of mustard. Fill the egg-white halves and enjoy a deviled egg.

924 **Make crazy cereal.** Pour just a little of every cereal in the cabinet into a bowl. Add milk and eat.

925 **Make no-shrimp cocktail.** Dip lettuce into cocktail sauce. Forget the shrimp.

926 **Make cheese popcorn.** Sprinkle warm popcorn with grated cheese.

927 **Make sweet popcorn.** Sprinkle warm popcorn with cinnamon sugar.

928 **Make an orange-banana salad.** Slice a banana. Peel an orange and cut it into sections. Mix the two fruits together, sprinkle with orange juice and a little honey.

929 **Invent a new sandwich.** Start with bread — the rest is up to you!

☆ TWISTED TONGUE TWISTERS TO TELL

See who can say the most twisters without getting twisted. Say each one five times.

930 Six slick sheiks.

931 How many cans can a canner can if a canner can can cans?

932 Betty Botter bought some butter, but she said: "This butter's bitter. If I put it in my batter, it will make my batter bitter. But a bit of better butter will make my batter better."

933 I saw Esau kissing Kate. Fact is, we all saw Esau. I saw Esau, he saw me, and she saw I saw Esau.

934 A tutor who tooted a flute tried to tutor two tutors to toot. Said the two to the tutor: "Is it harder to toot or to tutor two tooters to toot?"

✍ RIDICULOUS RIDDLES TO ASK

Don't just sit there twiddling your fingers. Fiddle with these riddles.

935 When is a car not a car?
When it's turning into a driveway.

936 What kind of town gets bigger as it gets smaller?
A ghost town.

937 What does a person have to know before teaching a pet tricks?
She has to know more than the pet!

938 If your aunt's brother is not your uncle, who is he?
Your father!

939 When does one and one make more than two?
When it's eleven.

940 What can you hold in your right hand but not your left hand?
Your left elbow!

941 What kind of witches go to the beach?
Sand-witches.

942 What's the difference between here and there?
The letter "t."

943 What do you call an annoying vampire?
A pain in the neck.

FUNNIEST BODY TRICKS TO PLAY

If you're looking for fun, and the only thing you've got up your sleeve is your arm, you're in luck! These funny tricks to play using your own body parts are sure giggle-getters.

944 **Disarm your friends.** Lean your shoulder against the doorway. Push your wrist as hard as you can against the frame as you count to fifty. Step away from the doorway and relax. Watch your arm float up all by itself.

945 **Try the All-Choked-Up trick.** Stand halfway in a doorway. Face into the room where people are. Grab yourself around the neck with one hand. Lean your head toward the open doorway and away from the hand that's grabbing your neck. Make it look as if you are trying to pull away from the hand, but can't. Struggle to get away, but don't. Stick your tongue out and act as if you're choking.

946 **Open wide and say, "Apple."** Try this impossible trick. Open your mouth wide and stick your tongue straight out so it's not touching your teeth or lips. Try to say "apple." You can't.

947 **Suck on your eyeball.** Your friends will say "Yeecchh!" when you do this. Pretend to remove one of your eyeballs with your fingers. Keep the eye you've "removed" closed. Pretend to put the eyeball into your mouth. Close your mouth and stick your tongue into your cheek. Move your tongue around so it looks as if the eyeball is in there rolling around. Pretend to take it out of your mouth and put it back in the eye socket. Lovely!

948 **Get your teeth knocked out!** Not really, of course. Blacken one or two of your front teeth with black eyebrow pencil. Go give someone a big smile!

949 **Get a giggle with Out-of-Control Arms.** Have a friend stand behind you and put his or her arms around your stomach. Put your arms around your own back so that your friend's arms are now where your arms were. Talk about anything you want and let your friend's arms and hands move along with your conversation. Your friend might scratch your head, stroke your chin, mess up your hair, push your cheeks together. Your friend's arms and hands are in control, but the laughter will be totally out of anyone's control.

950 **Stand on your knees and hold your feet up behind you with your hands.** Put a pair of shoes under your knees and try to move forward. It will look as if you've shrunk!

951 **If you have long hair, brush it all forward over your face.** Put on a pair of sunglasses and a hat.

Introduce yourself as Harry. If you have short hair, put a jacket on backward, put a hat on backward, and put a pair of sunglasses on the back of your head. Walk into a room and say, "I'm back!"

952 **Be two-faced and shock the world!** Leave one side of your face the way it is, and give the other side a totally creepy makeover. Cut out one egg cup from an egg carton. Cut a hole in the middle of it so you can see out of it when you put it over your eye. Color it red and place it over the eye. Use lipstick, eyebrow pencil or eyeliner pencil, or Halloween costume makeup to completely creepatize your face. Then sit quietly at your desk and call someone into your room. Sit with the "good" side of your face so the person will see it first. Then say in a sickly voice, "I feel kind of weird." As you slowly turn your face fully toward the person, say, "Do I look all right to you?" This one's a classic . . . in monster movieland, that is!

♥ PRACTICAL JOKES THAT GET 'EM EVERY TIME

Classics are things that have been around for a long time because they're really good. These practical jokes, or gags, are real classics. They've been fooling people for years.

953 **The old dollar-bill-on-the-string bit.** Tape an invisible thread or fishing line to a flat dollar bill. Leave the dollar bill on the floor. Hold the thread and stay out of sight. The first person to walk by is sure to bend down to pick up the buck. That's when you tug on the thread and watch the chase begin!

954 **Drool over dribble cups.** When a friend asks for a drink of water, hand over a paper cupful. When your friend sips, the water will dribble. How? Simple. Under the rim of the cup, poke small pinholes. Most people don't check their cups for leaks. Maybe after this they will!

955 **Easy gum, easy go.** Carefully unwrap all the sticks of gum in a five-stick pack. Take out the gum, refold the wrappers, and stick them back in the package. Go ahead. Offer a stick to someone. Surprise! It's a trick stick!

956 **String someone along.** Place a spool of thread in your pocket, leaving the end hanging down. Ask a friend to help you pull off the loose thread. Your friend will pull and pull and pull. You will laugh and laugh and laugh.

957 **Share a special box.** Cut a hole in the bottom of a small cardboard gift box. Stick your finger through the hole and cover it with cotton. Put the lid on the box. Ask a friend to open the box for a surprise. Don't *you* be surprised if your friend screams!

QUICK TRICKS FOR LAST LICKS

You'll always get the last laugh when you pull out one of these giggle-getting tricks. Go ahead, get 'em!

958 **You say:** "If a butcher is six feet two inches tall, what do you think he weighs?"
They say: "Huh? How should I know?"
You say: "He weighs meat!"

959 **You say:** "You look hungry. Want a Hertz Donut?"
They say: "What's a Hertz Donut?"
You say (giving a gentle punch on the arm): "Hurts, don't it?"

960 **You say (to an adult):** "How many kidneys do you have?"

They say: "Two."

You say: "Wrong! You don't have any kid-nees, only adult knees."

961 You say: "I bet I know what the last thing was that you took off before going to bed last night."

They say: "Impossible."

You say: "You took your feet off the floor!"

962 You say: "I can tell you exactly how many leaves are on that tree."

They say: "No, you can't."

You say: "Yes, I can. All of them!"

963 You say: "I'm so upset. I lost my henway."

They say: "What's a henway?"

You say: "Oh, about five pounds!"

964 You say (gently holding onto one of the other person's ears): "Do you want this ear any longer?"

They say: "Of course I do!"

You say: "Good, maybe pulling on it will make it longer!" (Then tug gently!)

965 You say: "If I can tell you the date, will you give me that coin you're holding?"

They say: "Sure, but you'll never be able to guess it."

You say: "The date is April 1" (or whatever today's date is).

966 You say: "I bet I can jump higher than the house."

They say: "Ha! Go ahead and jump."

You jump just a little bit and wait to see if the house jumps.
Then you say: "There. See? I jumped higher than the house jumped!"

☆ THE BOREDOM-BUSTER BAG

Don't leave home without it. When you run out of jokes to tell, games to play, and stuff to collect, dig into a busy bag. Take it along whenever you think you're going to be stuck — in line, at somebody's house, at a restaurant, or at the dentist's. Here are some suggestions for what to stash in your bag.

967 This book.

968 A mirror. There might be somebody behind you that you want to watch. You might need to decipher a backward message.

969 Empty bags to gather treasures.

970 A deck of cards. Whether you're solitary or with a crowd, you can always be a card if you keep a deck on hand.

971 Markers, paper, and pen.

972 A joke book.

973 One or two hand-held game boards.

974 A ball or two in different sizes.

975 Matchbox cars.

976 Chewing gum.

977 Graph paper for coloring squares while waiting around.

978 A rubber bug. Very good for startling people.

979 A quarter. In case you need to make a phone call or call heads or tails.

WHAT *NOT* TO DO IF YOU'RE SUPERSTITIOUS

Be safe, not sorry. Share these superstitions with your friends.

980 Never whistle in a theater. It's bad luck.

981 Don't fight with anyone on a bridge. You'll never make up.

982 Don't touch those scissors you dropped. Ask someone else to pick them up or you'll have bad luck.

983 Don't cross your knife with anyone else's at the table. You'll both have bad luck.

984 While you're at the table, don't spill any salt. Your day will be ruined.

985 Better not sleep at that table, either. You'll have bad luck when you wake up.

986 Keep your shoelaces tied. Your first piece of bad

luck might be tripping over them, and more bad luck may follow!

987 **Don't step on your own shadow.** Bad luck will shadow you.

988 **Don't look into a mirror with a friend.** You won't be friends much longer.

989 **Don't breathe when you pass a cemetery.**

990 **Don't walk under a ladder.** It's bad luck.

991 **Don't hop on the stairs on one foot.** You'll have bad luck when you get to the bottom.

✐ WAYS TO DO NOTHING WHEN THERE'S NOTHING TO DO

Let everyone else run around doing 991 weird things. Relax. Veg-out. Be a do-nothing.

992 **Try being a cat.** Tuck your paws in and curl up on a chair in a sunny spot by the window.

993 **Rock but don't roll.** Rock back and forth in the family rocking chair.

994 **Blow one bubble.** Lie down in the grass and watch your bubble float away.

995 **Bird-watch.** After your bubble floats away, keep lying in the grass. Stare at the sky and see how many birds fly over you in the next fifteen minutes.

996 **Stay still.** Don't move a muscle for ten minutes.

997 Don't do any of the Rainy Day activities (#150–#164). Just watch the rain fall instead.

998 Climb a tree. Watch the world go by from up there.

999 Lie down between two trees. Even better if there's a hammock in between!

1,000 Stare at the ceiling.

10 OF *YOUR* BEST IDEAS OF WHAT TO DO

What do you most like to do when there's nothing to do?

1,001   **List ten of your own suggestions:**

1. _____

2. _____

3. _____

4. _____

5. _____

6. _____

7. _____

8. _____

9. _____

10. _____